D0788046

Miss NIERGARTH
131 CHOICE ST,
CITY.

HOMAGE

HOMAGE

RECIPES AND STORIES FROM AN AMISH SOUL FOOD KITCHEN

CHRIS SCOTT

with Sarah Zorn

Photographs by Brittany Conerly

CHRONICLE BOOKS

SAN FRANCISCO

Text copyright © 2022 by **846 MERCHANT LLC.**

All rights reserved. No part of this book may be reproduced in any form without written permission from the publisher.

Library of Congress Cataloging-in-Publication Data

Names: Scott, Chris (Chef) author. | Zorn, Sarah, author. | Cornerly, Brittany, photographer.
Title: Homage : recipes and stories from an Amish soul food kitchen / Chris Scott with Sarah Zorn ; photographs by Brittany Cornerly.
Description: San Francisco : Chronicle Books, 2022. | Includes index. | Summary: "A narrative cookbook with 100 Amish Soul Food recipes"-- Provided by publisher.
Identifiers: LCCN 2021058073 | ISBN 9781797207742 (hardcover)
Subjects: LCSH: Amish cooking. | Cooking, American. | LCGFT: Cookbooks.
Classification: LCC TX721 .S46 2022 | DDC 641.5/66--dc23/eng/20211130
LC record available at https://lccn.loc.gov/2021058073

Manufactured in China.

Photographs by **BRITTANY CONERLY.**
Food styling by **JUDY KIM.**
Prop styling **MAEVE SHERIDAN.**
Design by **LIZZIE VAUGHAN.**

Bigelow's Constant Comment is a registered trademark of R.C. Bigelow, Inc.; Camel is a registered trademark of Reynolds Brands Inc.; Carolina Gold rice is a registered trademark of Riviana Foods Inc.; Cheerwine is a registered trademark of Carolina Beverage Corporation; Chick-fil-A is a registered trademark of CFA Properties, Inc.; Coca-Cola is a registered trademark of The Coca-Cola Company; Cocoa Krispies is a registered trademark of Kellogg North America Company; Crisco is a registered trademark of B&G Foods North America, Inc.; Crystal hot sauce is a registered trademark of Baumer Foods, Inc.; Entenmann's is a registered trademark of Bimbo Bakeries USA, Inc.; Kandy Kakes is a registered trademark of Tasty Baking Company Corporation; Hostess is a registered trademark of Hostess Brands, LLC; IHOP is a registered trademark of IHOP Restaurants LLC; Jell-O is a registered trademark of Kraft Foods Group Brands LLC; Kool-Aid is a registered trademark of Kraft Foods Group Brands LLC; Krimpet is a registered trademark of Tasty Baking Company Corporation; Old Bay is a registered trademark of McCormick & Company, Incorporated; Pop Rocks (POP ROCKS®) is a registered trademark of Zeta Espacial S.A. Company; Quaker is a registered trademark of The Quaker Oats Company; Ritz is a registered trademark of Mondelēz International; Sara Lee is a registered trademark of Sara Lee TM Holdings, LLC; Sazón Goya is a registered trademark of Goya Foods, Inc.; Swirly Cupkakes is a registered trademark of Tasty Baking Company Corporation; Tasty Klair Baked Pies is a registered trademark of Tasty Baking Company Corporation; TastyKakes is a registered trademark of Tasty Baking Company Corporation; *Top Chef* is a registered trademark of Bravo Media LLC; Tostitos is a registered trademark of Frito-Lay North America, Inc.; Triscuit is a registered trademark of Intercontinental Great Brands LLC; Wawa (plural Wawas) is a registered trademark of Wild Goose Holding Co., Inc.; Wesson is a registered trademark of Richardson Oilseed Products (US) Limited; Ziploc is a registered trademark of S. C. Johnson & Son, Inc.

10 9 8 7 6 5 4 3 2 1

Chronicle books and gifts are available at special quantity discounts to corporations, professional associations, literacy programs, and other organizations. For details and discount information, please contact our premiums department at corporatesales@chroniclebooks.com or at 1-800-759-0190.

Chronicle Books LLC
680 Second Street
San Francisco, California 94107
www.chroniclebooks.com

DEDICATION

THIS IS FOR MY CHILDREN,

ALI, PEARL, CALEB, AND NOA.

OUR FAMILY IS OUR STRENGTH, AND THE ONE WAY
I KNOW FOR SURE that we'll always remain
connected is through our food. As long as we
HAVE AND RESPECT THAT, we'll always keep each
OTHER. I'm counting on you all to make
Nana's Roly Polys at least once a year. she
would be happy to know that it still brings
US JOY. And every New Year's Eve or New
Year's day — make the oxtails, Black-eyed peas
and Shrimp Cocktail. This entire Book is
a love letter from Nana and Carmen to you,
through me. It's unfortunate that they passed
away before you got to know them.
THEY WERE STRONG, THEY WERE BEAUTIFUL,
AND THEY WERE CERTAINLY RESILIENT. THEY
HAD LOVE IN THIER HEARTS, AND I BET ALL
THE MONEY IN THE WORLD THAT YOU FOUR
WOULD HAVE BEEN THE BEST THINGS TO EVER
HAPPEN TO THEM.

ENJOY THE BOOK: USE IT UNTIL IT'S
CRUMBLING FROM THE SPINE AND GET
BACON GREASE ON A FEW PAGES.
It's ok — it's meant to be Used.

LOVE YOU.

DAD

GRANDPOP SUMNER BROWNE
AND HIS MOTHER, MAE BROWNE

421

GRANDMA HOWARD,
NANA, AND ME

GRANDPOP AND ME

A LETTER FOR US, TO US: SURVIVING THE TRANSITION

When things stabilize into something that resembles "normalcy," what will you have learned about yourself? What will you have learned about your world? I've asked myself this question many times recently, and now I present it to you.

In 2020, George Floyd, Breonna Taylor, and Rayshard Brooks were murdered by police just a few weeks apart from one another. For many, their deaths, along with a growing number of other racially motivated killings, were a starting point to discuss radical change. But I've seen hundreds of senseless deaths in my lifetime. And I've felt the same helplessness that I imagine my grandparents felt when they witnessed lynchings and beatings take place over and over and over again. It's made me wonder if I was destined to just live out my life watching Black people being murdered, and wonder if and when I'd be next.

All forms of racial injustices have been magnified, because of the calm in the midst of the coronavirus. I watched my people get sick because they had continued to work throughout the pandemic, as garbage workers, bus drivers, grocery store clerks, and restaurant workers. Often without health insurance. Pushing aside any mental health issues. Black men in particular carry around so much stigma and weight, a fear of being vilified or looked down upon for expressing fear, hurt, anxiety, despair, or pain.

The pandemic forced us to really pay attention. Everything moving so slowly allowed us to finally acknowledge the moans and groans of our suffering planet from pollution and global warming, the injustices between peoples and cultures, and the blatant exclusion of certain races and sexes from sharing our stories of joy and suffering.

A spotlight has been shone on the inequities that exist in food media. The narratives of resilience and triumph that inevitably bleed into the food of Black and Brown people have long been ignored, and ignored with intent. Somewhere along the line, it became an unspoken rule that you could give voice to only three or four Black chefs at a time.

So what can we do to survive this transition and make this next stage a better one? Will we miss this opportunity for growth? Or will we finally create change?

As I get older, I'm realizing my potential to become a mentor, sharing not only my technical culinary skills but also my wisdom and experience to support the next generation. I've always been grateful for the trail of bread crumbs left behind by my elders, and I'm ready to drop a few myself. This time, more than ever, we need to listen to the advice and read the writings left behind, and strengthen our foundation based on lessons learned from our past and our present.

I often think of the Last Supper and wonder if they had any sense of how relevant that meal would still be today. It was a Passover meal, which signifies the liberation of the Israelites from slavery. It's a meal used to remember suffering and bondage. It is also a meal prepared with love and surrounded by calm, meant to nurture the bodies of friends and family who fight the good fight. For centuries, food has served as a bridge, allowing us to both memorialize our painful pasts and give weight to our sorrows, while also celebrating our resiliency, our triumphs, and the paths we forged to the other side.

And so, in this time of pain and uncertainty, I've returned to what I know: cooking. Cooking is political; I believe that completely. It allows us to discuss food systems, poor eating habits, food apartheid, sustainability, corporate and government influence, and personal responsibility. Among chaos, finding a road to peace, through food, can be an act of revolution. When society rebukes and rejects you, strengthening your mental health and spiritual safety, through food, can be an act of revolution. For me, food has always been a place where I both lose myself and find myself again. Food is my tool for healing.

INTRODUCTION

Elizabeth Howard was my great-great-great-grandmother. She lived her life as a slave in Rappahannock, Virginia, back in the mid-1800s. When her children, James and Mattie, were young, the Emancipation Proclamation was signed, abolishing slavery. I can't imagine what it must have been like for her. After hundreds of years, and generations of oppression, I don't know how any of them were able to embrace the idea of freedom without confusion or fear.

IT TOOK GENERATIONS TO BREAK THE SLAVE MINDSET. YET FREEDOM EVENTUALLY BRED INSPIRATION.

I'm certain that many former slaves were afraid to abandon the "safety" of the plantation, for fear of being murdered or kidnapped—or any other dire consequence that was mentally beaten into them in case they ever thought about escaping. And they probably felt responsible for the family, reluctant to desert the massa and force the family to tend to the escapee's work themselves. Then there's the question of *What do I do if I go?* There was no telling if they would land on their feet in a different part of the country with only the clothes on their backs, without job skills, and with limited opportunity.

For those who stayed in the South, farming remained a significant role in their lives, whether they worked for the same person who had enslaved them or took part in sharecropping. As for those with a new vision of the South, sure, they knew that they were free, but there was no one to welcome them to the land of freedom. They were strangers in a strange land, surrounded by whites who largely believed them incapable of surviving on their own.

Many freed slaves fell ill; many died from disease or starvation. Others ended up in contraband camps, often located near Union Army bases. The conditions were unsanitary and food supplies limited. Often the only way to leave the camp was to agree to go back to work on the very same plantations they had recently escaped. It took generations to break the slave mindset. Yet freedom eventually bred inspiration, along with a sense of brave hope to make a change.

Elizabeth's son, James, had ten children with his wife, Bettie Johnson. And of those ten, many followed in their ancestors' footsteps and worked the farms or railroads, became housekeepers, or manufactured clothing. Except for one, Clarence Howard, my great-grandfather. He journeyed north to Pennsylvania and took a job in a steel factory. He met a woman, Sarah Evans, and had three children: Lynwood, Clyde, and Pearl, whom I came to know affectionately as Nana. It is here that I join the story—a branch on a family tree improbably extending from the antebellum South to the heart of Pennsylvania Dutch Country.

When I was about seven, my parents sent me away from them in South Carolina to live with my mother's mother, Pearl (otherwise known as Nana, to whom this book is an homage), in Coatesville, Pennsylvania. They were in the middle of a difficult divorce, but times had been bad long before that.

When my father was home, he'd be drunk and they'd be arguing, or he'd be talking about other women or complaining about his business problems. And though I didn't put two and two together until much later, there was also a period during which my mother was making attempts on her own life. She'd take all these pills and lie in bed, and I thought she was sick. She'd tell me she was just going to take a nap, but I should check on her every now and then.

* **1908** Clarence's brother, Eugene, with his family. A former sharecropper, he became the groundskeeper for the University of Virginia.

* **1916** Clarence Howard, Nana's father. He lost his arm on the job, coupling trains.

* 1972 Me

And if I couldn't wake her up, to call Nana because she'd know what to do. So I'd sit by myself in the living room, watching TV or hanging out with the dog, and look in on her every couple of hours to see if she was breathing.

Even once my mom finally joined us in Coatesville, three or so years after I arrived, she was hard to be around. After what my father put her through, she was bitter, angry, and resentful; just beat down by depression and sacrifice. So Nana was who I continued to turn to, all through my childhood. She's the one who cared for and nurtured me. She's the one who brought comfort and joy into my world. Everything that was her I gravitated toward, and that included cooking.

Nana was an excellent cook, and it seemed as if she was always in the kitchen. My grandfather would usually be there with her, sitting quietly with a bottle of blackberry brandy and a pack of Camels and listening to the Phillies on the radio. Nana always made an extra place setting for every meal, for the guest who may or may not arrive. Because all were welcome in Nana's house. She'd feed you, of course, and let you take a bath if you wanted one. And there was always room on the couch, if you needed to lay your head down.

Now, you may think I had it easy, growing up in a quiet small town, the only child in a house with two elderly people. But Nana brought the kind of regimented continuity to my life that I craved. She taught me to dress myself and brush my own teeth. She made me get up early and go to church. She impressed on me the importance of work: washing the clothes, mowing the lawn, shoveling the snow, shoveling the neighbor's snow. Many years later, even at my own restaurants, I'd end up shoveling the storefronts next to mine after a storm. The guys in the kitchen would tell me, "That's dumb! What have they ever done for you?" But that's Nana in my ear. It's a living lesson in tending to others—one that I plan to pass on to my own children.

ALTHOUGH FOR MOST
PEOPLE SOUTHERN
FOOD CONJURES UP
INSTANT IMAGES OF
COLLARD GREENS
AND SHRIMP AND GRITS,
I'VE ALWAYS
UNDERSTOOD IT AS
DISTINCTLY REGIONAL.

Nana wasn't the type of person to let me just sit around. If I tried to come home after school, throw my bag on the floor, grab a bowl of cereal, and plop in front of the TV, she wasn't having that. She'd say, "You can finish your cereal and then do your homework. And if you don't do homework, trust me, I have a whole list of other things you can do."

Homework was never fun. And I wasn't eager to do yard work or wash clothes, either. But when it came to cooking, well, I could easily stay with her for hours. And a lot of times, that's exactly how long it took. Especially if she was baking. That was an opportunity to just go slow, and put all your attention on the task at hand. Because baking is less about timing—getting something out of the way so you can move on to something else—than it is about process.

Because it had been forty years since Clarence Howard settled in his chosen new home of Pennsylvania, Nana's kitchen included local staples like rice, spaetzle, and various forms of potato dumplings. And the Southern cooking styles and techniques he brought with him from Virginia became fused with culinary traditions from the Amish, the Dutch, and the Germans who had heavily populated this part of Pennsylvania. So although for most people Southern food conjures up instant images of collard greens and shrimp and grits, I've always understood it as distinctly regional. You'll find Creole inflections in the

NANA AT THE STOVE WHERE
I LEARNED TO COOK

Florida Panhandle, stretching all the way to Louisiana. In the Carolinas, there's the Gullah influence. Move out to Texas and you're hit with BBQ. In the Mississippi Delta region, you'll find imprints from Mexican migrant workers. And as you move north, from Virginia to Pennsylvania and even as far as Canada, you'll find Appalachian, Dutch, German, and Amish influences all uniquely intermingling. This is where you'll discover the origin of the cuisine I call Amish soul food.

✳ 1963 My mom with her brother, Sonny.

There are tons of writings about freed slaves and what they ate. Hundreds of stories about Black women and fried chicken. Words from New York to California about soul food and Southern cuisine, past, present, and future. But soul food doesn't begin and end in the South. It's constantly changing as individuals travel to different areas, and the communities and local agriculture that surrounds them become incorporated into their culture and their food. Amish soul food may sound like a newfangled creation, but it's based on the very real history that my family shares with so many others.

When I was growing up in Coatesville, the Black population was fairly small. And Black interaction with the Amish was almost nonexistent, unless you were working with them or patronizing one of their businesses. Yet Amish food and influence was everywhere, and my introduction to all of it began the day I was born. Most of the diners and restaurants feature shoofly pie, moon pies, pot pies, the fried dough slabs known as elephant ears, potato bread, potato dumplings, apple dumplings, and chicken corn soup. The dishes created in Nana's kitchen—as well as the other households that surrounded

✳ EARLY 1950S Meriam Harris (Aunt Dee Dee).

❋ LATE 1930S Aunt Mim and Aunt Sara Mae.

us—were a very natural extension of that influence. Amish food, soul food, and Amish soul food is about making the best of what you have. It's the way of the poor people.

Much as Black folk fled to the northeast to escape slavery, the Amish made their way to the United States to avoid religious persecution. And in both cases, they arrived with little more than the clothes on their backs. So they built their own homes and grew their own food. They had flour from grains, plus maybe some greens and beans. And if they were lucky enough to have protein, they used every part of it, making pig ears into scrapple or skin into cracklings. The Amish community and the Black communities may not have used ingredients the same way, but they shared the same resources. When they reached into the pantry, they came up with the same things.

It hasn't been a smooth journey to embracing this history and these traditions, and through them, my food. If everything that went into forming who I am— the good, bad, and ugly—was the root, I spent my early years as a chef throwing concrete on top of it, trying to hide who I was.

The fact that my mother never supported the idea of me cooking? Well, that had a lot to do with it. Even when I started experimenting as a kid—taking the

✳ 1950S Nana's sister-in-law, Aunt Winnie (the woman looking at the camera at the far back left of the photo, seated to the left of the man with his back to the camera), at a women's function.

whole pack of hot dogs she'd bought for the house to make for my friends, serving them with all sorts of spreads and fancy mustards—she'd be pissed. "Why are you wasting up all our food?" she'd demand. Or she'd complain that I made the house smoky as I perfected my recipe for "ginger chicken" roasted with ginger powder, lemon juice, and garlic.

So when I told her that instead of using my degree in English lit to become a teacher, I was going to pursue becoming a chef? Well. That did it for her. She didn't see how that could ever be a real career. She was convinced that I'd be financially dependent on her my whole life. So starting from the time I was nineteen, we pretty much didn't talk for years.

Eventually, when I was working professionally in Philadelphia, my mother ended up coming around to some of my restaurants. And in true form, she smack talked most of them—all those small, casual places—saying, "This isn't food," "This is garbage," or something along those lines. It wasn't until I got the executive chef position at Novelty, a real fine-dining establishment with white tablecloths and real china in a real dining room (my last position previous to

[THIS BOOK] IS ABOUT SHINING LIGHT ON A CUISINE THAT EMBODIES THE PASSAGE BETWEEN SLAVERY AND PRESENT DAY.

this was in a basement below a bar), that I sensed a shift. Not that she said anything directly to me after coming to eat with us. There was no actual praise. Just a noticeable absence of shit talking. She laughed. She smiled. She enjoyed a glass of wine with my aunts. And for me, that was as close to a seal of approval from my mother as I ever received.

As a result, I came to believe that working in European restaurants, with a focus on fine-dining techniques, was the only professional path worthy of attention and respect. So when mentors suggested that I open a soul food restaurant, that it would be successful in Philadelphia, I chafed at the idea. I'd be damned if I'd be a Black chef, taking the "obvious" route of doing fried chicken and ribs. I stubbornly dismissed who I was, in an effort to mold myself into something I wasn't. No wonder I couldn't find my own voice. And feeling so disconnected, so rootless, took its toll on me, both creatively and emotionally. So much so that I ended up turning to alcohol, to keep down the submerged hurts of my past that kept swimming to the surface.

It wasn't until I relented by looking inward, at where I've been and who I've hurt—including myself—that I was able to reevaluate and refocus and break open that concrete. And I found that root was still strong and still growing, so I figured it was time to nurture it and see what it was about. In it, I discovered the pain, struggle, and joy of my childhood and the unique food traditions of my ancestors, intermingling with my newly acquired foundation of European cooking techniques. By exposing the root, I finally found the culinary voice I have now.

✳ **1984** The whole family gathered for a funeral at my Aunt Dee Dee's house in Rappahannock. My mom didn't allow me in the photo because I showed up dressed as a Michael Jackson impersonator (everyone loved it but her).

The truth is that fifty years' worth of personal and professional education are just now beginning to shape me. When you attempt to find your voice while trying to "sing" like someone else, you can never hit the notes just right. It's only once you're able to look into who you really are that you can speak and act and do with a clear heart. It's only then that the noise coming out of your mouth actually becomes music.

This is my family's story, over seven generations of love, influence, pain, joy, and success, from Virginia to Pennsylvania to Brooklyn and beyond. This book isn't just about me or trying to "put my stuff" out there. It's about shining light on a cuisine that embodies the passage between slavery and present day. It tells of the individuals who had the courage to seek a better life, and of those who were there to support them in the journey, followed by the communities that were created. I am only a gatekeeper, and as long as I am here to hold the flame and tell the story, I will do so, loudly and proudly.

PANTRY

Your Amish soul food pantry won't be complete without the following ingredients.

BLENDED OIL

This is a blend of canola and olive oil, and we always had a bottle in our pantry when I was growing up. This was mainly because it was affordable, but also because it felt higher in quality than your basic Wesson cooking oil. Great for baking as well as cooking, it's a switch hitter in recipes of all sorts.

BUCKWHEAT FLOUR

This high-protein flour is made by grinding buckwheat into powder. As robust as the flavor is, it's very low in gluten, so when making pancakes or blini, you need to supplement it with other flours, such as all-purpose. I love using buckwheat flour for binding scrapple, rolling dumplings, or whipping up low-gluten crackers for snazzy cocktail events.

CAROLINA GOLD RICE

Fluffy and slightly sweet, this is a variety of African rice that was brought to the United States and popularized in the Carolinas. A staple during the antebellum era, and my childhood, a pot of this rice always sat at the ready on our stove for folks to grab when they got hungry.

CIDER VINEGAR

Unless I need a relatively flavorless acid that will fade into the background (like white distilled vinegar), this is my go-to vinegar. It has great fermented apple notes and just enough sweetness to lend itself wonderfully to either sweet or savory recipes.

CORNMEAL

This is a staple ingredient in both Southern and Amish cooking, and has American roots across the board. Black folks, Appalachian folks, and Native Americans all use cornmeal in a host of recipes, from hot-water cornbread and hoe cakes to polenta and pone. I love it as a thickener in scrapple, a coating for dumplings, and a main ingredient in some desserts. Its versatility is endless.

KOSHER SALT

Growing up, Nana Browne used iodized salt. Hell, my family members to this day still use iodized. Once I was exposed to professional cookery, I began to understand the subtleties and nuances of salt, and how kosher, with its coarse, wide grains, adds a delicate touch and highlights the flavors of whatever you put it on or in. Iodized is a bit bitter and straight-up salty. And while I often use it when making salt cures and brines, whenever I mention salt in a recipe, I'm referring to Diamond Crystal kosher salt unless otherwise noted.

LOUISIANA-STYLE HOT SAUCE

Let's get it straight: Crystal hot sauce is the best Louisiana-style hot sauce on the market. We—and when I say we, I mean Black folks—were all raised on this brand. We put it on everything: scrambled eggs, potato chips, pigs' feet, greens, and even cocktails. You name it, we hit it with Crystal. Its vinegary burn is unique from all the other brands. And if you open the refrigerator of any aficionado, you'll find a half-used bottle with the cap off and caked-on gooeyness on the tip. This is the sauce of choice.

MOLASSES

Back in the day, sugar was known as a luxury ingredient. That's why, when looking at old recipes, I can immediately tell if they were written by someone with money or poorer folk. When it came to the latter, molasses was the more commonly available sweetener. A breakfast for poor children in the nineteenth century would often consist of warm bread slathered with some form of molasses . . . and that's it. Nowadays, molasses is turned to for its specific culinary properties, rather than its affordability. A thick, dark syrup made from sugar beets, sugar cane, sorghum, or even yams, it lends an earthy smokiness to cookies, cakes, pies, and BBQ.

MUSTARD SEEDS

In addition to being the base of homemade, whole-grain mustards, these go into almost all of our pickles, chow-chows, and stewed fruits, and add depth to many of the broths and likkers found in Amish cuisine.

STONE-GROUND GRITS

In my family, if you had Quaker grits in your pantry, you got the side-eye and a firm talking-to. That's because they're par-cooked and dehydrated, which makes them "instant." Stone-ground grits are considered far superior by any respectable, grit-loving aficionado. You get that true corn taste, chewy texture, and round mouthfeel that pairs perfectly with melted butter or a nice, toasty, brown roux gravy.

CHAPTER 1

Seven Sweets and Seven Sours

Traditional Amish meals follow a set format. You have your proteins and your starches. Your breads and desserts. But most important of all, you have to have your sweets and your sours.

Like many hardscrabble communities, Amish folk primarily ate what they could grow and produce themselves. So no wonder pickling, canning, and preserving have such deep roots in the culture. Fruit was turned into jams, chutneys, and compotes. These are the "sweets." For "sours," the Amish are best known for chow-chow, a cooked, vinegared relish made from whatever could be salvaged from the garden before the last frost (Southerners also take credit for chow-chow, making it an obvious staple in African American households like mine). Corn is the most common variety, frequently served alongside stewed tomatoes and a variety of pickles, such as cabbage, beans, beets, or even eggs.

As commonplace a table setting as salt and pepper, sweets and sours are either eaten as is or used as condiments, sauces, or spreads. They are meant to lend balance to each dish—a custom that very well could have started as an analogy for life, about taking the sour along with the sweet. And there really are supposed to be seven of each on the table. Of course, regularly setting out all fourteen is a pretty heavy lift in modern-day, non-Amish households. But incorporating the sweets and sours on your table is a practice that's easy to adapt to one's lifestyle (as I've adapted it to mine). Every easy, one-pot recipe in this chapter can be made once

stored in your pantry or fridge, and used year-round to elevate even the most basic of meals.

This interplay of sweet and sour underlies everything I make. If I'm cooking a slow braise of pork or beef, I might pair it with tomato chow-chow, flavored with cloves or allspice to give it a wintry depth. If I'm working with fish, I know I'll want something light, bright, and acidic, like cabbage or corn. My wife is Korean, so kimchi (and various versions of it) has found its way into my repertoire as well. And I'll always think of Nana when I whip up a batch of prune compound butter. It's an homage to her regular snack of prunes, toast, and super-sweet tea.

The deeper I go in exploring Pennsylvania Dutch culture and my family's Southern history, the more I'm compelled to look at things in reverse and trace the migration of flavors all the way back. Back to before my people were slaves, to discover what they ate in the Caribbean (which is why I've started making Preserved Mango, page 43) or in South America, or back home in Africa . . . and how that's shaped what we eat now. So from Apple Butter (page 39) and Rhubarb Chow-Chow (page 50) to Sweet-and-Sour Green and Wax Beans (page 61) and Green Tomato Confit (page 59), every jar and bottle actually contains the story of the journey, of how the contents came to get there.

PRUNE COMPOUND BUTTER

1 cup [180 g] dried pitted prunes

⅓ cup [65 g] packed brown sugar

¼ cup [60 ml] fresh orange juice

1 Tbsp fresh lemon juice

½ tsp kosher salt

1 dash ground cloves

1 dash ground allspice

1 dash ground nutmeg

1 dash ground cinnamon

4 cups [904 g] butter, at room temperature

It was no secret that my Nana had a hardcore sweet tooth. One of her vices was hot tea (Bigelow's Constant Comment) and a couple of Pecan Rolls (page 225), accompanied by soft butter and a small dish of prunes. She'd smear the pecan rolls with the butter, top it with the prunes, and go to town.

As a nod to Nana, I made this butter our house butter at my restaurant Butterfunk Kitchen, served with the biscuits and cornbread. It always evoked a sense of calm in me, similar to what I felt watching her sitting there, collecting her thoughts with a pecan roll and some soft butter. She had an aura of peacefulness that just flowed into your spirit.

MAKES 9 CUPS [2 KG]   In a small saucepan, combine the prunes, brown sugar, orange juice, lemon juice, salt, cloves, allspice, nutmeg, and cinnamon. Add ½ cup [120 ml] of water and bring to a simmer over medium heat. Turn the heat to low and cook until thick and jammy, about 40 minutes. Place in a blender with the center cap off, draped with a kitchen towel (to let steam escape) and purée until super smooth. Let the purée cool to room temperature.

Add the purée to a mixing bowl along with the butter, and whip by hand or with a mixer until completely combined. Spoon into small mason jars or airtight containers, or use wax paper to roll the whole mass into a log. Store the butter in the refrigerator for up to 2 weeks or in the freezer, well wrapped, for up to 2 months. Bring to room temperature before using.

APPLE BUTTER

6 green apples, peeled and cut into chunks

¼ cup [50 g] granulated sugar

¼ cup [50 g] packed dark brown sugar

1 Tbsp vanilla extract

¾ Tbsp kosher salt

¾ Tbsp ground cinnamon

¼ tsp ground nutmeg

I don't think it's possible to grow up in the North without a deep appreciation of apples. I know I eagerly anticipated all the apple "somethings" Nana prepared during autumn, including the lovely apple butter that was normally right next to the regular butter on the kitchen table.

At one point in my career, though, I was too arrogant and fancy for such a "pedestrian" ingredient. If I was using apples, it was to make pectin, or sorbet, or something molecular.

It wasn't until I began my process of recovery and rediscovery that I gained a renewed respect for apples. The Bible describes the apple tree as symbolizing qualities we should strive to achieve in our daily lives: truthfulness, appreciation for beauty, and a remembrance of our past. Being raised by a godly woman like Nana, who articulated these qualities through everything she grew, ate, and touched, I couldn't help but bring apples (and this classic Pennsylvania Dutch condiment) back into my circle.

MAKES 1 QT [950 G]   In a large saucepan over medium heat, combine the apples, granulated sugar, brown sugar, vanilla, salt, cinnamon, and nutmeg. Cook the mixture until it releases liquids and comes to a boil, then lower the heat to low. Cook until thick and dark, about 1 hour. Purée in a blender until smooth, then cool to room temperature. Pour into sterilized jars or place in airtight containers. Store the apple butter in the refrigerator for up to 1 week or, if using sterilized jars (see sidebar, page 40), in the refrigerator for up to 6 months or in a cool, dark place for up to 2 months.

MINCEMEAT

2 cups [400 g] packed dark brown sugar

2 cups [280 g] diced beefsteak tomatoes

2 cups [280 g] peeled and diced green apples

2 cups [280 g] golden raisins

1 cup [140 g] black raisins

1 cup [220 g] beef suet or lard

Zest and juice of 2 lemons

3 Tbsp cider vinegar, plus more as needed

2 Tbsp candied lemon peel

2 Tbsp candied orange peel

2 Tbsp chopped hazelnuts

2 tsp ground cinnamon

½ tsp ground nutmeg

¼ tsp ground cloves

¼ tsp ground allspice

¼ tsp ground ginger

¼ tsp ground mace

3 Tbsp dark rum

1 Tbsp brandy

Nana would set this on the table as a condiment for meat or potatoes. Needless to say, it's also great as a filler for pie.

MAKES 3 QT [2.8 L]   Combine the sugar, tomatoes, apples, raisins, suet, lemon zest and juice, vinegar, candied citrus peels, nuts, and spices in a saucepan and cook over medium heat. Once bubbling, lower the heat to low. Cook, stirring occasionally, for 2 hours, or until the mixture gets a caramelized color. Be careful not to overly reduce, or you'll end up with mincemeat that's too thick, sweet, or burnt. If it begins to stick to the pot while cooking, add small amounts of water or cider vinegar.

After 2 hours, add the rum and brandy and cook for 10 minutes more. Remove from the heat and pour into sterilized jars or cool completely and place in airtight containers. Store the mincemeat in the refrigerator for up to 2 weeks or, if using sterilized jars (see sidebar), for up to 2 years.

HOW TO STERILIZE JARS

When placed in airtight containers, these sweets and sours will last from 1 to 2 weeks in the fridge. When you use the sterilization process, however, you can make an otherwise perishable product keep for 1 month to 2 years (as long as you don't open the top). Feel like getting your preserve on? The process is easy.

Wash glass jars and lids. Bring a large pot of water to a boil and submerge the lids and jars in the boiling water for 10 minutes. Remove from the water using tongs and drain well to remove excess water. Place the hot product in the sterilized jars, close the tops tightly, and let cool at room temperature before storing in a dark closet or pantry.

CONCORD GRAPE PRESERVES

6 cups [1.36 kg]
Concord grapes

3 cups [600 g] sugar

Peels from 3 lemons

1 Tbsp kosher salt

Mrs. Mitchum lived next door to us. She was around my grandmother's age, and you'd spy them chatting through the gate almost all the time during the warmer months. They were both avid gardeners and would spend hours cultivating their flowerbeds and vegetable gardens until they were picture-perfect. It was a bit of friendly competition between neighbors.

Nana grew green figs in our yard. She would often bring up the Bible verse from the book of Luke to me: "Jesus said that when the fig tree would blossom, the Kingdom of God was near." So being the ornery young teenager that I was, I was always nervous around that damn tree, fearing the day that the blossoms formed. But that's a story for another time.

Anyway, Nana would give Mrs. Mitchum a small bushel of figs, and she'd usually make a pie or some preserves. And in return, Nana would receive some gorgeous Concord grapes. Even to this day, the smell of Concord grapes brings back wonderful memories, especially when I use them to recreate the preserves that Nana used to make.

Note: Since I don't add pectin or excess sugar, the preserves have a looser texture than you might be used to. If you'd like a thicker jelly, combine 1 Tbsp of cornstarch with just enough water to make a slurry. Whisk into the preserves after they've cooked for 1 hour, and cook slowly over low heat for an additional 5 minutes.

MAKES 2 CUPS [600 G]   Rinse the grapes under cold water and slice in half to remove the seeds. Keep the skin on the grapes; it adds color and flavor.

Place the seeded grapes in a saucepan with the sugar, lemon peel, and salt. Cook over medium-low heat for 1 hour, stirring frequently to avoid sticking. After 1 hour, remove from the heat, remove the lemon peels, and let the preserves cool slightly.

While the preserves are still hot, ladle into hot sterilized jars (see sidebar, facing page). Top with sterilized lids and allow to cool completely. Store in the refrigerator overnight, then keep for up to 5 months at room temperature.

PRESERVED MANGO

2 mangos, peeled and diced (reserve the pits)

Juice and zest of 6 limes

¾ cup [150 g] packed brown sugar

¼ cup [40 g] kosher salt

¼ cup [35 g] jerk seasoning

1 Thai chile, minced

1 Tbsp toasted mustard seed

This is by far one of my favorite condiments, especially served with braised oxtail. But it pairs great with any type of meat or fish, or even grilled vegetables for that matter. The inspiration came to me when I began tracking the journey of my ancestors all the way back to Africa. Each flavor sort of represents a stop along the way, from West Africa through the Caribbean and parts of South and Central America, and eventually into North America. (For jerk seasoning, I like the Flair brand found at flairfoodevents.com.)

MAKES 1 QT [950 G]   Put all the ingredients (including the mango pits, which add flavor) in a large stainless steel bowl. Mix by hand vigorously, massaging all the ingredients into the mango. Add to a 1 qt [1 L] container and cover. Refrigerate for at least 3 days before using. The preserved mango will keep, refrigerated, for up to 2 months; after that, it becomes too goopy.

KIMMEL CHERRIES

4 cups [860 g] pitted sour
cherries

4 cups [960 ml] cider vinegar,
or enough to cover

2 cups [400 g] sugar

Summertime in Coatesville meant the emergence of Amish vendors, selling all of their farm-fresh goodies. You couldn't drive even half a block without passing the lovely roadside stands, where proud Amish families would lay out their kimmel cherries. I'm not sure why they're called "kimmel," actually; we just referred to them as sour cherries. These were great on almost anything, from ice cream to roasted pork. You were always bound to find a jar of cherries on our dinner table. And preparing them yourself is tremendously easy. You only need four things: cherries, vinegar, sugar, and time.

MAKES 4 CUPS [960 G]   In a large nonreactive bowl, add the cherries and enough cider vinegar to just cover them and let sit for at least 10 hours and up to 24 hours. Pour into a colander and let drain for 1 hour.

Combine the cherries and sugar in a large nonreactive bowl. Cover with a cloth and store in a cool place for 1 week. It normally takes this long to dissolve the sugar without applying heat, and this length of time also adds flavor to the finished product. Store the cherries in sterilized jars indefinitely, or in airtight containers in the refrigerator for up to 1 week.

YAM MOLASSES

1 large African yam, peeled, peel reserved

2 small sweet potatoes, peeled, peel reserved, coarsely chopped

1 pound [455 g] dark brown sugar

2 Tbsp kosher salt

1 Tbsp ground allspice

1 tsp freshly cracked black pepper

1 fresh bay leaf

Not to be confused with smooth, orange sweet potatoes, yams have rough skins and white, fibrous flesh; they are the centerpiece of many African dishes. Over the years, I've thought of all the different ways Nana used to prepare sweet potatoes so I could try them with yams instead. This molasses proved a bit of a brilliant brain wave—if I do say so myself. Because yams are sweet (but not too sweet), the starches act as a natural thickener, and roasting them promotes that dark, deeply earthy flavor associated with molasses. This is also a pretty dead-on example of the way I'm constantly trying to track my lineage through food, starting with Africa (yams), leading to the American South (sweet potatoes), and ending up with molasses, courtesy of the Pennsylvania Dutch. The flavor is very potent and a delicious complement to everything from meat to bread to dessert.

MAKES 2 CUPS [480 ML]   Preheat the oven to 350°F [180°C]. Roast the yam until tender, about 40 minutes.

Coarsely chop the roasted yam and add with the sweet potatoes and both peels to a large Dutch oven or heavy-bottomed pot. Fill with enough water to cover the tubers by 1 in [2.5 cm]. Add the sugar, salt, allspice, pepper, and bay leaf to the pot, cover, and bring to a boil over high heat. Lower the heat to medium, remove the lid, and simmer for 1 hour.

Use a hand strainer or spider to remove all the tubers and peels from the liquid and discard them. Return the liquid to medium-low heat and simmer slowly to reduce, until the mixture becomes thick as molasses and dark brown but still translucent, about 1½ hours. The starches from the tubers should be enough to thicken the liquid, but you can make a cornstarch slurry to help it along if need be. Store in an airtight container, refrigerated, for up to 2 months.

CHOW-CHOW,
THE KING OF CONDIMENTS

When it comes to American relishes, chow-chow rules them all. Well, according to southerners and the Pennsylvania Dutch, that is. In the South, you'll see chow-chows made from finely diced bell peppers and onions and occasionally tomatoes or beans. In the North, it's predominantly cabbages and corn. The British have a version of this called piccalilli, which is similar to Indian pickles. But in the end, it's the same damn thing, just done with different ingredients.

One of my favorite things to do at Amish markets is look through the varieties of chow-chow. It's like a kaleidoscope of colors—purple cabbage, red beets, and green and yellow beans, seasoned with grain mustard or horseradish. Then there's my personal favorite, corn. It's super sweet but with a satisfying crunch, almost like nature's Pop Rocks.

In many respects, I'm a purist, passionate about keeping and preserving techniques and traditions, to obtain the very same results that my ancestors got. But my chef side is always urging me to push the envelope, and chow-chow provides the perfect playground for experimentation. So I ended up developing a few new versions, bound to knock your wool socks off.

RHUBARB CHOW-CHOW

3 cups [600 g] sugar

2 cups [480 ml] white vinegar

½ cup [70 g] finely diced white onion

½ cup [60 g] finely diced green bell pepper

2 Tbsp kosher salt

2 tsp dry mustard

2 tsp mustard seeds

8 cups [960 g] coarsely diced rhubarb

You can go the sterilized jar method with this relish (see sidebar, page 40), but I prefer to refrigerate it in airtight containers. That's because the longer this chow-chow is hot, the more the rhubarb breaks down and turns mushy. That's not a bad thing—it's just not as pretty.

MAKES 1.5 QT [1.4 L]   Combine the sugar, vinegar, onion, bell pepper, salt, mustard, and mustard seeds in a large stainless steel saucepan. Simmer over medium-low heat for 20 minutes. Add the rhubarb and continue to cook for about 15 minutes more, or until just tender. Be careful not to overcook, or the rhubarb will turn to stringy mush. Remove from the heat, pour onto a baking sheet, and refrigerate immediately to cool it down. Store in airtight containers in the refrigerator for up to 1 week. *Note:* Any excess liquid is great for use in vinaigrettes or marinades.

OKRA CHOW-CHOW

1½ cups [360 ml] white vinegar

15 spears large fresh okra, thinly sliced

½ red bell pepper, seeded, deribbed, and finely diced

½ yellow bell pepper, seeded, deribbed, and finely diced

½ red onion, finely diced

⅜ cup [75 g] sugar

1 Tbsp kosher salt

2 Tbsp chopped, fresh parsley

A sweet-and-sour symmetry is inherent in my style of cooking. If it isn't expressed through actual components of a dish, it's delivered via side bowls or ramekins. Okra chow-chow has become one of my favorite media for attaining culinary harmony. And considering that okra is integral to Southern cuisine and agriculture, it's also one of the clearest examples of two food cultures existing side by side and the ways they intersect. Serve okra chow-chow alongside scrapple (as I so often do), and you could consider this dish the poster child of Amish soul food.

MAKES 3 CUPS [900 G]   Place the vinegar, okra, bell peppers, onion, sugar, and salt in a small pot over medium heat. Simmer, uncovered, until the mixture reduces by half and just starts to thicken, about 45 minutes. Remove from the heat and let cool. Stir in the parsley and refrigerate until ready to use, up to 6 months.

UNDERSTANDING OKRA

Many folks dislike the slimy texture of okra. But you can actually make that slime work for you. One thing I do is sear the okra in a very hot pan in small batches, until the slime essentially caramelizes. Another trick is soaking sliced okra in salted vinegar before cooking it—30 minutes to 1 hour will usually do the trick. Then just take it out of the salted vinegar, give it a rinse, and pat dry before cooking or doing whatever you're going to do.

YELLOW TOMATO AND SORGHUM CHOW-CHOW

6 cups [960 g] coarsely chopped yellow or red tomatoes

2 cups [400 g] sugar

2 cups [480 ml] white vinegar

3 small white onions, finely diced

1 red bell pepper, seeded, deribbed, and finely diced

¼ cup [40 g] kosher salt

1 tsp turmeric powder

1 tsp mustard powder

1 tsp ground cloves

1 tsp mustard seed

1 tsp ground allspice

½ cup [90 g] cooked sorghum grain

I love drawing inspiration from what my own family grew and ate. But it's also important to me to pay respect to African farmers from long ago, whose crops and husbandry skills were spread by the diaspora through the American South and straight to home cooks like my grandmother.

The fifth most important cereal crop grown in the world, sorghum grain can be used as is or transformed into anything from molasses to beer to bread. I love the texture it brings to this unique condiment, contributing a pea-like snap and chew to a stew of sweet yellow tomatoes.

MAKES 2 QT [2 L]   In a large stainless steel saucepan, add the tomatoes, sugar, vinegar, onions, bell pepper, salt, and spices. Bring to a simmer over medium heat and cook for 40 minutes to 1 hour, stirring often to avoid sticking. You want the final product to be slightly syrupy and viscous.

One you have reached this point, add the cooked sorghum and cook for 10 minutes more. Remove from the heat and immediately store in glass jars using the sterilized canning technique (see sidebar, page 40), or let cool and store in airtight containers in the refrigerator for up to 1 week.

BREAD-AND-BUTTER PICKLES

15 kirby cucumbers, thinly sliced

2 Tbsp kosher salt

1 white onion, thinly sliced

1½ cups [360 ml] cider vinegar

1 cup [200 g] granulated sugar

½ cup [100 g] brown sugar

1½ Tbsp mustard seeds

1½ tsp celery seeds

⅛ tsp turmeric powder

It's easy to automatically associate pickles with cucumbers. Not only are they the first pickles many of us taste, but they're also often the first we actually learn to create. And they teach us the fundamentals that allow us to expand our understanding of pickles later on.

You first learn to make a brine, tweaking it as needed to achieve the sweet-and-sour balance that gives the pickle its taste. And you learn what produce goes well with what preparation; for instance, Nana would never use anything but small, sturdy kirbys for her bread-and-butter pickles. This recipe is a great introduction to the process. Master this, and the world is your (pickled) oyster.

MAKES 4 CUPS [1.2 KG]   In a large mixing bowl, combine the cucumbers and salt. Cover and refrigerate for 2 hours. Transfer the cucumbers to a colander and rinse and drain well. Discard any liquid left in the bowl. Place the cucumbers back in the bowl along with the onions and mix to combine.

In a large saucepan, combine the vinegar, granulated sugar, brown sugar, mustard and celery seeds, and turmeric and cook over medium heat until the sugar dissolves, about 2 minutes. Pour the hot mixture over the cucumbers. Let sit at room temperature for 1 hour. Cover the bowl and refrigerate for 24 hours. Store in airtight containers in the refrigerator for up to 1 month.

GREEN TOMATO CONFIT

6 green tomatoes, quartered and thinly sliced

1 red onion, thinly sliced

2 cups [400 g] sugar

¼ cup [20 g] whole coriander seed, toasted and then ground

2 fresh bay leaves

2 fresh makrut lime leaves, or the peel of 1 lime

2 Tbsp kosher salt

1 cup [240 ml] white vinegar

Olive oil to cover

When we used to serve this at my restaurant, we'd keep the tomatoes stored in the confit oil until ready to plate. The whole kitchen crew couldn't help but put a little bit on everything we snacked on. It went on our eggs in the morning. We'd slather it on our toast. We'd eat it with a family meal, whatever the family meal was. It was the perfect kitchen condiment. I deeply recommend keeping some handy in your own refrigerator for everyday use.

MAKES 3 QT [2.8 L]   Preheat the oven to 300°F [150°C].

Put the tomatoes, onion, sugar, coriander, bay leaves, lime leaves, salt, and vinegar in a stainless steel mixing bowl and toss to thoroughly coat the tomatoes. Pour into an even layer in a 9 by 13 in [23 by 33 cm] baking dish. Add the olive oil to just cover, wrap tightly with aluminum foil, and roast for 3½ hours.

Remove the foil and let cool at room temperature. With a slotted spoon or a kitchen spider, transfer the tomatoes from the oil into sterilized jars (see sidebar, page 40) to store for up to 1 month or airtight containers to store for up to 10 days. Top with just enough oil to cover. Refrigerate until ready to use, and serve cold or at room temperature.

SWEET-AND-SOUR GREEN AND WAX BEANS

8 oz [230 g] green beans

8 oz [230 g] yellow wax beans

1 cup [120 g] thinly sliced red bell peppers

1 cup [120 g] thinly sliced yellow bell peppers

1 red onion, thinly sliced

1 cup [240 ml] olive oil

1 cup [240 ml] apple cider vinegar

⅓ cup [65 g] sugar

3 Tbsp chopped fresh dill

2 Tbsp Dijon mustard

1 Tbsp kosher salt

When it came to Nana's garden, pole beans were one of the crown jewels. And she was adamant about trimming only the end that was attached to the vine. See, if you pick off both ends, you create a passageway in the bean for hot steam and liquid to pass through when cooking. If you trim off only one end, then most of the cooking happens on the outside, leaving the natural flavors, juices, and fibers inside of the bean intact.

Shocking the bean in ice water extends its life even further. So you can prepare this 24 hours before a cookout and leave it to marinate, and it still looks like you made it that day.

MAKES 2 CUPS [455 G] Bring a large pot of water to a boil and prepare an ice water bath. Add the beans to the water and cook for 30 seconds, or until they turn bright green. Immediately transfer to the ice water to stop the cooking process. Drain the beans well, then transfer to a large bowl with the peppers and onions. In a small bowl, mix together the oil, vinegar, sugar, dill, mustard, and salt. Pour over the vegetables and let sit for at least 3 to 4 hours or overnight. Portion into sterilized jars (see sidebar, page 40) for indefinite storage at room temperature or airtight containers for up to 1 month. Store the wax beans in the refrigerator for up to 2 months after opening.

OLD BAY COLESLAW

3 cups [720 g] mayonnaise

1⅓ cups [265 g] sugar

1 cup [140 g] shredded carrot

1 cup [60 g] shredded red cabbage

1 cup [60 g] shredded white cabbage

1 cup [240 ml] white vinegar

1 red onion, thinly sliced

¾ cup [220 g] Old Bay seasoning

1 Tbsp kosher salt

I've served this to guests who proclaimed themselves to not be coleslaw people, and they inevitably ended up taking seconds. Now, my lovely wife believes that the level of seasoning in this recipe is a little out of hand, so she makes a version with a little less sugar and Old Bay. Go on and make this my way, or pull back a bit and make it hers; it'll be another level in our friendly competition called Battle Coleslaw!

MAKES 6 CUPS [1.4 L]   Mix all the ingredients in a large bowl until well combined. You can eat this right away, but it's best to let it sit overnight in the refrigerator to really develop the flavor.

AN ODE TO MR. HOLMES

Back home in Coatesville, there's a local mini market chain called Turkey Hill. They're basically countrified Wawa stores. And as you walk along the counters, you'll come across big glass jars filled with pickled pigs' feet and, right next to them, a big ole jar of some damn near purple pickled eggs, with plastic tongs hanging off the side.

Where I'm from, pickled eggs are a treat. You'd grab a couple on your way to school or after track practice, or perhaps your mother would send you to buy a couple jars for the next backyard BBQ. Even the smaller markets would sell them. There was a place called Holmes Store Market at the end of my block. It was actually a front for a weed spot, but you could go and buy some penny candy, a bag of chips, or pickled eggs. Mr. Holmes—a smooth Black brother and proprietor of the market—would make his pickle brine extra spicy. All the old heads would frequent this place to pick up beer, weed, and a couple of super-spicy pickled eggs. Come to think of it, by adding his own funky twist to a traditional Pennsylvania Dutch treat, Mr. Holmes might have been an early adopter of Amish soul food cuisine.

CHAPTER 2

All Day, E'ery Day

My grandfather was a truck driver, delivering produce and dairy from Philly to Hoboken and all the way to New York City. It sounds like a pretty respectable job, but for a Black man, from the late 1930s to the early 1960s, it had its challenges. This was during segregation, mind you, so he was never allowed to stop and eat at any of the places he made deliveries to. Most of these places wouldn't allow him to use the restroom, let alone sit and purchase something to eat or drink.

White truck drivers would damage or deflate the tires on my grandfather's truck, to slow him down and jeopardize his job. They would sometimes mess with his products as he removed them from the truck, such as replacing his full boxes with empty ones. Now and then they would even lay hands on him, trying to provoke a fight.

Grandpop found the path of least resistance and frequented stops that were friendly to Black motorists during his deliveries. After dropping off the dairy and produce, he'd go to safe places to refill on gas, lay his head down for a quick nap, or sit down to eat somewhere he could share a laugh with kindhearted individuals. When I opened my restaurant Sumner's Luncheonette, I tried to create the kind of place where he would have liked to have been a regular. A place where he could take a break, have a chat, and get a bite. From breakfast through lunch and an afternoon snack, the recipes in this chapter are dishes I know he'd gravitate to on a menu.

It's been interesting to observe the all-day, luncheonette-style concept growing in popularity again. Not that it's all that surprising. Like they were in my grandfather's time, these are spots where you're guaranteed to find filling, affordable food that isn't too fussy, along with a (relatively) diverse cross-section of people.

These places give folks the opportunity to refuel and connect, despite their busy lives. The only thing asked of anyone is to simply show up and sit down. Luncheonettes also allow people to stop the clock for a while, to eat whatever speaks to their own personal schedule, be it Country Ham Steak (page 80) for breakfast, Egg Salad with Bread-and-Butter Pickles (page 68) at lunch, or perhaps a bowl of Spicy Pimento Cheese (page 87) with Buckwheat Crackers (page 203) at any time, as a restorative snack to help catapult them to the next part of their day.

I definitely appreciate the breakfast-all-day nature of luncheonettes, because weekday breakfasts were never a big thing in my house growing up. My mother was normally up and out of the house by 4:30 or 5 a.m. Snow days were the worst—she would make me wake up with her so I could dig out her car, so she could get to work on time. I would normally fend for myself when it came to breakfast: a slice of toast or a bowl of a high-sugar cereal did the trick, if I ate anything at all.

We were simply too busy to be worried about eating in the morning. Many of my childhood friends also suffered when it came to breakfast, and as I grew into adulthood, I realized this was an epidemic in the Black community. Many low-income kids don't eat breakfast at home due to overextended parents and super-long commutes that take up all of their time. Speaking for myself, I know that as soon as I'm awake, I hit the ground running. I've been groomed to feel like stopping and eating is cutting into my time frame, even though I try to encourage a good breakfast for my kids.

Like my mom was, I'm a working parent, and I worry that the habits she ingrained in me could rub off on them. So more and more, I try to make feeding my family my first and foremost priority, no matter what. Even if it's just on the weekends or during holidays, it's great to sleep in and wake up to a nice meal—like the incredible Nana Browne's Fried Potatoes and Onions (page 70), which you can smell cooking before you even open your eyes. Eating breakfast together always makes my family feel more like family. And I hope you'll find a few recipes here that help you deepen the bond with yours.

JOHNNYCAKES WITH APPLE BUTTER

1 cup [140 g] all-purpose
flour

1 cup [140 g] cornmeal

2 Tbsp sugar

2½ tsp baking powder

1 tsp kosher salt

2 eggs

¾ cup [180 ml] milk

⅓ cup [80 ml] melted butter

1 tsp vanilla extract

¼ cup [60 ml] vegetable oil,
plus more as needed

Apple Butter (page 39), for
serving

Served with Jerk Pork (see page 73) and corn chow-chow, these little corncakes were one of the most popular appetizers at Butterfunk Kitchen. But they also have a sweet side. When smeared with Apple Butter (page 39), one of the go-to Seven Sweets and Sours in Amish Country, Johnnycakes make for one terrific breakfast.

SERVES 4 Sift together the flour, cornmeal, sugar, baking powder, and salt into a medium mixing bowl. Add the eggs, milk, ½ cup [120 ml] of water, the butter, and vanilla and whisk until smooth and combined.

Put a cast-iron skillet or sauté pan over medium-high heat and add the oil. When the oil is hot, scoop about 2 Tbsp of batter per cake into the pan, making mini pancakes.

Fry until brown on one side, about 2 minutes. Use a spatula to flip and brown the other side. Continue cooking the pancakes in batches, adding more oil to the pan if needed. Serve immediately with apple butter.

EGG SALAD WITH BREAD-AND-BUTTER PICKLES

4 large hard-boiled eggs, peeled and chopped

1 celery stalk, finely diced

1 green onion, thinly sliced

3 Tbsp chopped fresh parsley

3 Tbsp mayonnaise

1½ tsp fresh lemon juice

1 tsp Dijon mustard

Kosher salt and freshly cracked black pepper

4 slices toasted white bread, for serving

Bread-and-Butter Pickles (page 58), for serving

Lettuce and sliced tomatoes (optional)

This is the trick Nana had up her sleeve when we kids whined about being hungry. It's quick and easy, and she generally had all the ingredients on hand, so she could whip it up in a pinch. You'll definitely want to keep a supply of bread-and-butter pickles at the ready so you can whip it up in a pinch too!

SERVES 2   In a medium bowl, combine the chopped eggs, celery, green onion, parsley, and mayonnaise. Add the lemon juice, mustard, and salt and pepper.

Divide the egg mixture evenly among two pieces of toast. Top with pickles, lettuce, and tomato and the other two slices of toast. Slice each in half and serve immediately.

CRISPY POTATO WAFFLES

4 russet potatoes, peeled and cut into large chunks

2 tsp fresh lemon juice

1 onion, cut into large chunks

6 eggs, beaten

3 Tbsp flour

3 Tbsp cornstarch

2 Tbsp chopped fresh parsley (optional)

2 tsp kosher salt

1 tsp freshly cracked black pepper

I wanted to come up with my own distinctive waffle recipe. Amish folk are all about potatoes, so this seemed like a no-brainer; it's basically a crispy, savory potato pancake, pressed into a waffle shape. You can top these with whatever dried seasoning you'd like, dip them in ketchup, ranch dressing, or hot sauce, or even smear with a dollop of Chicken Liver Mousse (see page 188). Now how do you like dem waffles?

MAKES 8 WAFFLES   Preheat the oven to 200°F [90°C].

In a food processor, purée the potato completely. Add the lemon juice and pulse to combine. Pile the potato purée onto a cheesecloth or clean kitchen towel, pull the edges up around the purée to make a hobo bundle, and squeeze out the excess water over the sink. Put the purée in a large stainless steel bowl and set aside.

Add the onion to the food processor and purée until totally smooth. Transfer to the potato bowl, along with the eggs, flour, cornstarch, parsley, salt, and pepper. Mix everything together until well combined.

Spray a waffle maker with nonstick spray. Prepare the waffles according to the manufacturer's instructions. The waffles can be kept warm on a baking sheet in the oven while you work.

NANA BROWNE'S FRIED POTATOES AND ONIONS

4 Tbsp [50 g] bacon fat, butter, or olive oil

2 Tbsp unsalted butter

2 russet potatoes (about 1 lb [455 g]), washed and sliced into ¼ in [6 mm] rounds

¼ tsp kosher salt

¼ tsp freshly cracked black pepper

Chopped fresh herbs, such as thyme and rosemary (optional)

1 Vidalia onion, thinly sliced

Without a doubt, this is one of the top five dishes I associate with Nana, and the one that, despite how simple it is, I have the hardest time replicating (believe me, both my wife and I have tried). Maybe that's because it owes as much to memories as it does to technique. The smell of it would lure me from my sleep: sweet onions and potatoes, fried crisp in the bacon fat that Nana would collect in a can beside the stove (she threw nothing away). Making these was a pure expression of love for her family and the best possible way for us to start our day.

SERVES 4 In a large skillet over medium-high heat, melt the bacon fat and butter. Arrange about half of the potatoes evenly over the surface of the pan. Try not to over-lap them if you can help it, since it's important to get a good crispy sear on the surfaces. Sprinkle the salt, pepper, and herbs, if using, over the top. Top with the sliced onion, then top the onion layer with the rest of the potatoes and cover with a lid.

Once the bottom layer of potatoes is golden brown and has a nice sear, about 8 minutes, turn the layers over so the top layer of potatoes are on the bottom. It's perfectly fine to flip it in bits; don't worry about executing one perfect flip. Once the bottom potatoes are golden brown, scoop portions onto serving plates and serve immediately.

CHEESE GRITS WITH JERK PORK

FOR THE PORK AND BRINE

½ cup [120 ml] dark rum

¼ cup [50 g] brown sugar

3 Tbsp soy sauce

3 Tbsp kosher salt

2 Tbsp molasses

1 Tbsp Worcestershire sauce

1 Tbsp minced fresh ginger

1 tsp ground allspice

½ tsp ground cinnamon

One 5 lb [2.3 kg] bone-in pork shoulder

FOR THE JERK MARINADE

3 cups [720 ml] fresh orange juice

1 cup [240 ml] dark rum

1 white onion, quartered

¼ cup [60 ml] cider vinegar

¼ cup [60 ml] olive oil

2 whole Scotch bonnet peppers

4 garlic cloves, crushed

2 Tbsp fresh thyme leaves

2 Tbsp fresh lime juice

1 Tbsp brown sugar

FOR THE CHEESE GRITS

2 cups [480 ml] chicken broth

2 cups [480 ml] whole milk, plus more as needed

4 Tbsp [55 g] butter

½ tsp garlic powder

1 cup [140 g] stone-ground grits

1½ cups [120 g] shredded Cheddar cheese

Kosher salt

These grits are Nana all the way. And the jerk pork pays homage to Black folk who came here from the Caribbean, bringing their culinary traditions with them. Together, they're the perfect expression of the way I cook: interweaving the influences of those who came before me. *Note:* You'll need to start this at least a day in advance.

SERVES 4   *To make the pork:* In a large measuring cup, combine the rum, brown sugar, soy sauce, salt, molasses, Worcestershire, ginger, allspice, and cinnamon with 3½ cups [840 ml] of water. Stir until the salt and sugar dissolve. Put the pork in a large bowl and pour the brine over the pork. Cover with plastic wrap and refrigerate for at least 4 and up to 6 hours.

To make the marinade: In a blender, purée the orange juice, rum, onion, vinegar, olive oil, peppers, garlic, thyme, lime juice, and brown sugar. Remove the pork from the brine and pat dry. Discard the brine. Using a fork or knife, poke holes in the pork butt and pour the marinade over the top. Cover and refrigerate the pork for 24 hours.

cont'd

Prepare a grill for indirect cooking over medium-low heat, 325°F [165°C]. Remove the pork from the marinade (reserve the marinade) and place on the cool side of the grill with the fat cap facing up. Cover the grill and cook, basting every 30 minutes with the reserved marinade, for roughly 2½ hours, or until the internal temperature reaches 190°F [90°C] in the center and the juices run clear. Remove from the grill and let cool slightly.

To make the grits: In a medium saucepan over medium-low heat, combine the broth, milk, butter, and garlic powder (the liquid should have some flavor before adding the grits). Bring to a simmer.

Increase the heat to medium-high and gradually add the grits, whisking continuously. Whisk until the grits are smooth and creamy but still toothsome, about 30 minutes. You can add more milk if they get too thick. Turn off the heat, add the cheese, and whisk in until combined. Season with salt and set aside, covered, until ready to use.

When the pork is cool enough to hand shred, place some on top of a bowl of cheese grits, and serve warm.

VARIATION

To make buckwheat grits, follow the same recipe but use 1 cup [240 ml] more chicken broth and add ½ cup [90 g] of buckwheat groats or kasha with the grits. I especially like using this in my version of head-on shrimp and grits.

RICE FOR BREAKFAST

I can't think of one culture in which rice isn't a major staple. I have Haitian friends who put out elaborate dishes when it's time to eat, but it's all incomplete without that plate of rice. When I was working for the celebrated chef Michael Solomonov back in Philadelphia, he taught me how to make rice in the Israeli way, stressing the importance of the tahdig—the panfried, crispy layer of rice crust at the bottom of the pot. He would share stories of his own family with me, and how this part of the rice dish was one of his favorites.

Rice was also a big staple in my house when I was growing up. As much as Southern cooking is associated with grits, Nana would always have a small pot of buttered rice on the stove with the lid on. You could help yourself anytime you wanted and eat it as is, or splash a little hot sauce on it, or grab something from the fridge and add it to your bowl of rice.

When we opened Butterfunk Kitchen, guests were always confused as to why we served rice with everything, instead of the expected biscuits and cornbread. It was important for me to show how my family actually ate, and what we actually ate, which was rice with every single meal. How it was a part of my culture, just like it is for my Haitian and Israeli friends. Rice is everything.

When I met my wife, Eugenie, she would prepare for me a lovely breakfast dish called gyeran bap, featuring leftover rice from the rice cooker (being Korean, she ate rice with every meal too). It's quickly stir-fried in a pan until crispy, seasoned with sesame oil and soy sauce, topped with any leftover meat and vegetable from the night before, and served with a fried egg on top. It's delicious and truly the one dish that describes our love and our relationship. Thirteen years later, she still makes this dish for me and our children in the morning. She'll switch it up sometimes, depending on the weather, by making a rice porridge with a little fish stock and spinach leaves.

I'm proud to be living and eating my way through many cultures based on just this one ingredient: rice. I've always said, if you really want to understand a culture, eat their bread. Well now, I think I need to add rice to that story.

CRISPY "CITY MOUSE" SCRAPPLE

1 lb [455 g] pork butt, cut into large chunks

¼ cup [60 ml] vegetable oil

Kosher salt and freshly cracked black pepper

2 smoked ham hocks

2 bunches fresh sage

2 celery stalks, halved

1 onion, quartered

1 carrot, peeled and halved lengthwise

⅓ cup [105 g] molasses

1 tsp ground allspice

1 tsp ground cloves

1 tsp freshly cracked black pepper

5 cups [700 g] cornmeal

1 cup [140 g] buckwheat flour

White flour, for dredging

Butter or bacon fat, for frying

Okra Chow-Chow (page 51), Pimento Cheese Spoonbread (page 206), or poached eggs (see sidebar, page 78), for serving

Sit down to a slice of Nana's scrapple, and you'd end up picking bits of bone out of your teeth. But that was just part of the game. She used ears, snout, cheek, liver, and heart in her scrapple, thickened it with cornmeal, and pan-seared it so it stayed nice and gooey inside.

I'll admit to using fewer pig parts than Nana would, so consider this my "city mouse" version of a very country dish. I start with a savory cut, like shoulder or butt, and add in some ham hocks for smokiness. The fine folks of Pennsylvania eat scrapple mostly for breakfast, seared and served with an egg, some ketchup, or syrup. I've found that with just a tiny bit of chef-like tinkering, it's yummy (and dare I say, even sort of elegant) all day, e'ery day! *Note:* This dish must be started a day ahead.

SERVES 12 TO 16 Preheat the oven to 400°F [200°C].

Place the pork butt in a large baking dish. Coat evenly with the vegetable oil and season with salt and pepper. Roast until caramelized, about 35 minutes.

Add the caramelized pork to a large stockpot, along with the ham hocks, sage, celery, onion, carrot, molasses, allspice, cloves, cracked pepper, and cold water (12 cups [2.8 L] or enough to cover the ingredients). Cover the pot and bring to a boil over high heat. Lower the heat to a simmer and cook until fork-tender, 3 hours more.

Set a colander over a large pot or heatproof bowl. Drain the cooked solids through it and reserve 12 cups [2.8 L] of the liquid (if you have less than 12 cups, add some salted water to make up the difference).

cont'd

Discard the vegetables and finely chop or purée the meat. Add the meat and the 12 cups [2.8 L] of liquid to a large pot and bring to a boil. Lower the heat to medium and slowly whisk in the cornmeal and buckwheat flour. Once it binds to become a tight mush, transfer to an ungreased, 9 by 13 in [23 by 33 cm] baking dish. Smooth the top and refrigerate for 24 hours until completely set.

After 24 hours, remove the scrapple from the baking dish and slice into 2 by ¼ in [5 cm by 6 mm] squares. At this point, you can wrap any extra squares in ziplock bags, freeze, and then defrost once ready to use.

Dredge slices of scrapple in the flour. Add the butter or bacon fat to a cast-iron or heavy-bottomed pan, heat over medium heat, and add the scrapple squares in a single layer, working in batches if needed. When golden brown and crispy (about 4 minutes per side), remove from the pan and pat dry with paper towels. Serve with your favorite accompaniments, such as Okra Chow-Chow or Pimento Cheese Spoonbread and poached eggs.

HOW TO POACH AN EGG

Fill a small saucepan with at least 3 in [7.5 cm] of water. Add 1 tsp of salt and 2 tsp of white vinegar. Bring to a simmer over medium-low heat. Using a slotted spoon, stir the water until a vortex forms. While the water is swirling, crack one egg into the vortex. Cook for 2½ minutes, or until the whites are just firm enough to encase the yolk, but the yolk remains jiggly. Use the slotted spoon to lift out the egg and place it on a plate or on your composed dish. Repeat with remaining eggs.

SCRAPPLE:
THE ULTIMATE AMISH TREAT

Just as the Scots get mocked for haggis, the mid-Atlantic affinity for scrapple has become a bit of a running gag. Except among those who are actually from there, of course. Not only does everyone eat it, but everyone enjoys it—and not in an ironic way. Toddlers are pretty much weaned on scrapple. I remember my aunts feeding bits of it to my baby cousins, and I'm sure I came up on it too. Every diner in the area serves scrapple, every grocery store sells processed scrapple, and I think it's safe to say scrapple is in 75 percent of homes from South Jersey to Pittsburgh. It certainly played a big role in mine.

Early Amish folk were poor but entirely self-sufficient, a way of being that's very much in line with the slaves' circumstances. The "waste not, want not" mentality was strong in both communities and remained so for generations after. Both groups knew how to take even the most seemingly unsavory parts of the hog and turn them into something delicious.

COUNTRY HAM STEAK WITH FRIED EGGS AND PEPPER CABBAGE

2 cups [400 g] packed brown sugar

½ cup [160 g] molasses

2½ Tbsp pink curing salt

1 Tbsp pickling spice

One 7 lb [3.2 kg] boneless picnic pork shoulder

Fried eggs and Pepper Cabbage (page 95), for serving

On occasion, Grandpop would get his hands on a big ole 7 lb [3.2 kg] pork picnic shoulder. And Nana would know exactly what to do with that: make ham! Keep in mind that we come from a large family, so 7 lb [3.2 kg] of meat didn't go all that far, especially since Nana would fix up plates for the next-door neighbors too. That was her: always with her mind set on sharing and a heart full for people who needed to eat.

Now, you can skip a lot of these steps by simply purchasing a center-cut ham steak. But for me, there's nothing like going through the motions of the cooks who came before me, especially those who couldn't depend on all our modern-day conveniences. It makes me feel like a part of something larger and connects me to my ancestors in a way that nothing else does. *Note:* You can use two smaller shoulders instead of one big one. Just make sure to adjust the smoking time accordingly. This dish must be started 3 days ahead.

SERVES A CROWD OF FAMILY, FRIENDS, AND NEIGHBORS, WITH LEFTOVERS   In a large, sanitary tub that will fit into your refrigerator, combine the sugar, molasses, curing salt, and pickling spice. Bring 2 qt [2 L] of water to a boil and pour it into the bucket. Stir until combined. Add 4 qt [4 L] of cold water to the bucket and stir. Add the pork. Make sure the pork is totally submerged; you can do this by placing weights on top of it. One easy way is to place ziplock bags filled with water in a pie pan on top of the meat. Loosely cover and allow to brine in the refrigerator for 3 days.

Rinse the ham very well under cold water and pat dry. Prepare a smoker grill and heat to 225°F [110°C]. Smoke for 8 to 10 hours (or for two smaller hams, 4 to 5 hours), until the internal temperature reaches 160°F [70°C].

Slice off a nice hunk of ham, leaving the fat cap on. In a frying pan over high heat, sear the ham well on both sides until caramelized, about 6 minutes per side.

Serve with sunny-side-up eggs and pepper cabbage.

GRANDPOP'S MEATLOAF SANDWICH
WITH CARAMELIZED ONION RELISH

FOR THE MEATLOAF

3 eggs

¾ cup [180 ml] milk

¾ cup [105 g] bread crumbs

2 lb [910 g] ground beef

½ cup [70 g] finely diced onions

3 Tbsp plus 1 cup [160 g] ketchup

1 tsp plus 3 Tbsp hot sauce

2 Tbsp chopped fresh parsley

1 tsp dried oregano

1 tsp dried thyme

2 Tbsp brown sugar

FOR THE RELISH

3 Tbsp vegetable oil

2 red onions, julienned

¼ cup [50 g] packed brown sugar

¼ cup [60 ml] apple cider vinegar

2 Tbsp chopped fresh parsley

1 Tbsp chopped fresh rosemary

4 tsp kosher salt [23 g]

2 tsp freshly cracked black pepper

FOR SERVING

Toast

Sandwich spread (your favorite; Grandpop preferred mayonnaise)

Lettuce

Tomatoes (optional)

Grandpop used to take me everywhere with him, like to the store to buy his cigarettes. I just thought he liked the company, but it wasn't until much later that I learned I was his eyes. His sight was going, but he was too proud to either admit it or go to the doctor. So he'd take me by the hand, and I was the way he retained his link to the world. The upshot was that we became inseparable, and since this sandwich was one of his favorite dishes, it quickly became mine.

SERVES 8   Preheat the oven to 350°F [180°C]. Spray an aluminum foil–lined baking sheet with nonstick spray.

cont'd

To make the meatloaf: In a mixing bowl, combine the eggs, milk, and bread crumbs. Let sit for 5 to 10 minutes, until the crumbs have mostly absorbed the liquid. Add the ground beef, diced onions, 3 Tbsp of the ketchup, 1 tsp of the hot sauce, the parsley, oregano, and thyme. Mix until just combined. Form the mixture into an 8 by 4 in [20 by 10 cm] loaf on the prepared baking sheet. Bake for 40 minutes.

Meanwhile, combine the remaining 1 cup [160 g] of ketchup, remaining 3 Tbsp of hot sauce, and the brown sugar. After the first 40 minutes of baking, spread this mixture on top of the meatloaf. Bake for an additional 10 to 15 minutes or until the loaf is cooked through and the internal temperature reaches 160°F [70°C]. Let rest for 10 minutes before slicing.

To make the relish: While the meatloaf is baking, in a skillet over high heat, heat the vegetable oil. When just about smoking, add the julienned onions. Quickly toss the onions in the pan and cook until tender, about 5 minutes. Add the brown sugar, vinegar, parsley, rosemary, salt, and pepper and lower the heat to medium. Simmer until slightly thick and syrupy, about 4 minutes. Remove from the heat and let cool to room temperature.

To serve: For each sandwich, sear a slice of the meatloaf in a skillet, crisping both sides. Spread the toasted bread with sandwich spread. Assemble each sandwich by topping a slice of toast with a seared meatloaf slice, then caramelized onion relish, lettuce, sliced tomatoes, and another slice of toast. Serve immediately.

CREAMED CHIPPED BEEF WITH BROWN MILK GRAVY AND TOAST

6 Tbsp [85 g] butter

⅓ cup [45 g] all-purpose flour

1 tsp freshly cracked black pepper

1 tsp sugar

1 tsp onion powder

3 cups [720 ml] milk

5 oz [140 g] air-dried beef, such as Hormel brand or Italian bresaola, torn into pieces (Nana sometimes used pastrami for special occasions)

Thick-sliced toast, for serving

Nana always referred to this dish as "brown milk toast." She'd refuse to acknowledge it if it was listed at a diner as creamed chipped beef or whatever. And besides, there was no need to order it since she was such an expert at making it herself, as it was on the list of fifteen-some-odd dishes that Grandpop always craved.

Brown milk toast was part of the wordless routine they performed with each other. Grandpop would sit at the kitchen table, smoking his Camels, drinking his blackberry brandy, and listening to his Phillies. Nana would put his toast in front of him, he'd eat it, she'd clear it, and then he'd go and fall asleep in his living room chair for the rest of the day.

SERVES 2   In a cast-iron skillet over medium heat, melt the butter until bubbling. Stir in the flour, pepper, sugar, and onion powder and cook, stirring, until it forms a light brown roux. Add the milk and whisk until the flour is fully incorporated and the mixture is thick. Add the meat and stir until evenly coated. Spoon over the toast and serve.

THE CHEATER'S GUIDE TO MAKING ROUX

Now, I'm not going to step on the real, laborious way to make a roux. I'm talking about that combination of butter and flour that you stand over and stir until it's white, then blond, then a shade of brown that's just this side of burnt. If you're after a roux that actively contributes to taste, like in a gumbo, that's the only way to go.

But when it comes to roux that's only meant to act as a thickener, like in mac 'n' cheese or creamed chipped beef, I'm all about taking the cheater's way out. In a mixing bowl, whisk together regular flour and oil to make a slurry. Whisk this into your hot (must be hot) liquid. Keep whisking to the desired thickness, being mindful to "cook" the flour.

BOILED PEANUT HUMMUS

2 smoked ham hocks

2 cups [455 g] shelled, unsalted peanuts

1 tsp sugar

1 tsp kosher salt, plus more as needed

1½ tsp white vinegar

¼ cup [55 g] tahini paste

2 Tbsp fresh lemon juice

2 tsp ground cumin

2 tsp garlic powder

¼ tsp ground cayenne pepper

2 Tbsp extra-virgin olive oil

Freshly cracked black pepper

Buckwheat Crackers (page 203) or roasted vegetables, for serving

Grown throughout the Carolinas, Georgia, Northern Florida, Alabama, and Mississippi, peanuts play a major role in Southern agriculture. And while much of the country enjoys them raw or roasted, southerners are much more likely to prepare them boiled. You end up with an amazing, nutty potlikker that can be sipped straight up, or used to flavor other dishes. The potlikker certainly enhances this regional play on the popular Middle Eastern spread.

Southerners take a lot of knocks for having an unhealthy food culture, but if you look at their longtime reliance on farming, you'll see it's not necessarily so. They just know how to make things especially delicious. And served with roasted vegetables or Buckwheat Crackers (page 203), this hummus could almost be considered downright virtuous—yet I'm willing to bet my pork-loving Southern ancestors would approve.

MAKES 3 CUPS [680 G]   In a large pot, combine the ham hocks, peanuts, sugar, ½ tsp of the salt, ½ tsp of the vinegar, and 4 cups [960 ml] of water. Cover the pot and bring to a boil over medium-high heat. Lower the heat to medium-low and simmer until the peanuts are tender, about 1½ hours.

Discard the ham hocks. Strain the peanuts, reserving the cooking liquid.

In the bowl of a food processor, add the peanuts, tahini, lemon juice, cumin, garlic powder, cayenne, the remaining ½ tsp of salt, and the remaining 1 tsp of vinegar. Add ¾ cup [180 ml] of the cooking liquid. Purée to form a smooth paste. With the motor running, slowly drizzle in the olive oil until incorporated. Add more of the cooking liquid if needed to achieve your desired consistency. Season with kosher salt and pepper.

Serve warm or cold with buckwheat crackers or roasted vegetables, and store any leftover hummus in the refrigerator for up to 10 days.

SPICY PIMENTO CHEESE

2 cups [160 g] shredded extra-sharp Cheddar cheese

8 oz [240 g] cream cheese, cubed, at room temperature (cut cubes when the cheese is cold)

4 oz [115 g] roasted red peppers, drained and chopped

¼ cup [60 ml] white vinegar

3 Tbsp mayonnaise

¼ tsp garlic powder

¼ tsp onion powder

¼ tsp Old Bay seasoning

¼ tsp blackening seasoning

Kosher salt and freshly cracked black pepper

Toast points, Ritz or Triscuit crackers, sliced baguette, or biscuits for serving

This is a standby snack. And if you keep a big bowlful in the refrigerator like Nana did, there's no end of ways you can use it and enjoy it. Serve with toast points, with Triscuits or Ritz crackers, or (as I do nowadays) generously smeared in a grilled cheese or a patty melt.

MAKES 2 CUPS [455 G]   In the bowl of a food processor, combine the Cheddar, cream cheese, peppers, vinegar, mayonnaise, garlic powder, onion powder, Old Bay, and blackening seasoning. Blend until smooth and thick, about 30 seconds. Season with salt and pepper. Serve immediately with toast points and crackers alongside, or refrigerate in an airtight container for up to 1 week, letting it come to room temperature if you'd like it to be spreadable.

DEVILED HAM

8 oz [225 g] coarsely chopped Country Ham Steak (page 80) or store-bought ham

4 oz [115 g] cream cheese, at room temperature

¼ cup [60 g] mayonnaise

2 Tbsp chopped fresh parsley

1 Tbsp sweet pickle relish

2 tsp whole-grain mustard

2 tsp hot sauce

1 green onion, chopped

1 tsp fresh lemon juice

Kosher salt and pepper

Toast points, Ritz or Triscuit crackers, sliced baguette, or biscuits, for serving

Whenever company was coming over, deviled ham was invariably on the menu. Nana would lay out a bowl of it alongside crackers and pimento cheese, and she and Grand-pop would play cards and pinochle with their friends, while old jazz music warbled in the background.

MAKES 4 CUPS [900 G]   In the bowl of a food processor, combine the ham, cream cheese, mayonnaise, parsley, pickle relish, mustard, hot sauce, green onion, and lemon juice. Blend until smooth and thick, about 30 seconds. Season with salt and pepper.

Serve immediately with toast points and crackers alongside, or refrigerate in an airtight container for up to 7 days. Bring to room temperature before serving.

CRISPY FRIED CORN ON THE COB WITH BUTTERMILK RANCH

FOR THE BUTTERMILK RANCH DRESSING

½ cup [120 ml] buttermilk

⅔ cup [160 g] mayonnaise

⅔ cup [160 g] sour cream

¼ cup [60 ml] white vinegar

3 Tbsp sugar

1 Tbsp garlic powder

1 Tbsp onion powder

1 Tbsp chopped fresh chives

1 tsp chopped fresh dill

1 tsp chopped fresh parsley

Kosher salt and freshly cracked black pepper

FOR THE CORN

Vegetable or canola oil, for frying

4 ears corn, shucked and silk removed, tips trimmed if necessary

3 egg whites

1 cup [140 g] cornmeal

2 Tbsp Old Bay seasoning

1 tsp kosher salt

Bacon bits or crispy chicharrón, for topping (optional)

This is inspired by the memories of the county fairs in Coatesville. My spin on this classic treat is to smother it in creamy, tangy buttermilk ranch. Needless to say, the dressing is a real switch-hitter, so make a lot, and use it as a dip, salad dressing, or a coating for catfish before frying.

MAKES 4 EARS OF CORN   *To make the buttermilk ranch dressing:* Combine all the ingredients in a blender or whisk in a mixing bowl.

To make the corn: In a deep fryer or a Dutch oven, add enough oil to come halfway up the sides of the corn. Heat the oil to 350°F [180°C]. Line a plate with paper towels.

In a large bowl, whisk the egg whites until they are frothy. Roll the corn in the egg whites, covering the kernels completely.

In a wide, shallow dish, whisk together the cornmeal, Old Bay, and salt. Dredge the corn in this mixture, turning it to coat on all sides.

Add the corn to the hot oil and cook until golden brown, 2 to 3 minutes. Using tongs, remove the corn from the oil and transfer to the paper towel–lined plate to drain. Season with salt. Drizzle some buttermilk ranch on the corn, top with bacon bits, if desired, and eat while hot.

CRAWFISH HUSHPUPPIES WITH OLD BAY REMOULADE

FOR THE OLD BAY REMOULADE

¾ cup [180 g] mayonnaise

2 Tbsp chopped sweet pickle relish

2 Tbsp sugar

1½ Tbsp Old Bay seasoning

1½ tsp apple cider vinegar

1 tsp grated horseradish

FOR THE HUSHPUPPIES

Vegetable oil, for frying

1½ cups [360 ml] buttermilk

1½ cups [210 g] all-purpose flour

1 cup [140 g] cornmeal

4 oz [115 g] thawed and drained crawfish, roughly chopped

¼ cup [50 g] sugar

1 egg

1 Tbsp plus 1 tsp baking powder

1 Tbsp Old Bay seasoning

1½ tsp garlic powder

¼ tsp Sazón Goya seasoning salt

This recipe was passed down by my aunts, but it was my wife, Eugenie, who perfected it. She thought the hushpuppies were too dense, and she swapped in crawfish for the original shrimp to jazz it up. The result? We went through thirty to forty orders at my restaurant each day.

MAKES 25 TO 30 HUSHPUPPIES   *To make the remoulade:* In a medium bowl, whisk together the mayonnaise, pickle relish, sugar, Old Bay, vinegar, and horseradish. This can also be made ahead of time and will keep, refrigerated, for up to 1 month.

To make the hushpuppies: Add enough oil to come halfway up the sides of a Dutch oven or heavy-bottomed pot, and heat over medium-high heat until it reaches 350°F [180°C]. Preheat the oven to 200°F [90°C]. Line a plate with paper towels.

In a large mixing bowl, whisk together the buttermilk, flour, cornmeal, crawfish, sugar, egg, baking powder, Old Bay, garlic powder, and Sazón. Let sit for 5 to 10 minutes to thicken up.

Using a tablespoon, scoop balls of the batter into the oil, keeping them submerged while cooking (do not allow them to float). Fry for 3 to 5 minutes, until golden brown outside and fully cooked but still tender within. Using a slotted spoon, transfer to the paper towel–lined plate to drain. Put the finished hushpuppies on a baking sheet in the oven to keep warm.

Repeat with the rest of the batter, checking the oil periodically to make sure it maintains a temperature of 350°F [180°C]. Serve with remoulade on the side.

CHAPTER 3

Greens, Beans, Tubers, and Grains

A mish soul food is so much more than just a collection of side dishes. This chapter dives deep into another primary building block of our food: local agriculture. As I mentioned earlier, the Pennsylvania Dutch community and my Southern ancestors subsisted on whatever they were able to grow themselves. For the most part, and in both instances, that consisted of greens, beans, tubers, and grains.

When a southerner mentions greens, they almost always mean collards. Turnip and beet greens are widely used, but collards are king, for sure. Part of the draw—at least initially—is how nutritious they are. During slavery, when collards were being cooked, the masters would take the greens and cede the leftover cooking liquid, or potlikker, to the slaves, not realizing they were leaving the vitamins and nutrients behind. The same went for beans: Much of the actual sustenance remained in the cooking liquid in the pot. So whether consumed solo, or flavored with whatever scraps of meat they were able to keep, the nourishing potlikker from greens and beans was one key food the slaves relied on to survive and thrive.

Flour, corn, rice, and various other grains like sorghum and millet fleshed out the rest of their diet. And these are what Nana based most of our meals on too—a reliance that anyone who's ever needed to stretch a buck to feed their family will recognize. A pot of rice was always available to us, and a bit of flour or potato could be transformed into spaetzle or dumplings, which she'd sear in butter and serve with a little grated cheese, or use as a base for those collard greens or black-eyed peas. Nowadays, these dishes would generally be considered sides to the main event. But to us—and our ancestors before us—they formed a cheap and satisfying meal.

NANA BROWNE'S COLLARD GREENS

2 pig's feet, split in half

2 smoked ham hocks

4 smoked neck bones

½ cup [120 ml] white vinegar, plus more if needed

¼ cup [50 g] sugar, plus more if needed

3 Tbsp kosher salt, plus more if needed

2 lb [910 g] collard greens

Hot vinegar sauce, for serving

In Black culture and society, you are absolutely judged by how you cook your collard greens. Friends and relatives will barge into your kitchen, stick their heads into your pot, and give you either the side-eye or a half-hearted compliment.

The likker is the true spirit of the collards. It's the potion of a million ancestors all in one broth. And it contains all the nutrients cooked out of the leaves and stems. I usually keep some of this likker to use in other recipes. Collard green potlikker is gold.

SERVES 12 In a large pot over high heat, add the pig's feet, ham hocks, neck bones, vinegar, sugar, and salt, along with 10 cups [2.4 L] of water, and bring to a boil. Lower the heat to medium and cover. Let cook until the meat is falling off the bone and the potlikker has thickened, about 40 minutes. At this point, you can adjust the seasoning with more vinegar, salt, or sugar if you like, but this proportion should be pretty spot-on.

Wash the collards. Roll each leaf up like a cigar and cut into 1 in [2.5 cm] thick strips, stems and all. Add the greens to the pot, making sure they're submerged in the potlikker.

Cover the pot and cook for 2 hours. Fish out the pig's feet, ham hocks, and neck bones, being careful not to leave any small, loosened bones behind in the pot. Pick as much meat as you can off of the bones, and coarsely chop the meat. Return the meat to the pot of greens and stir.

Serve with a few dashes of your favorite hot vinegar sauce.

PEPPER CABBAGE

12 Tbsp [170 g] butter or lard

¼ cup [60 ml] white vinegar

3 Tbsp kosher salt

12 whole peppercorns

1 bay leaf

½ tsp baking soda

1 head green cabbage, stem attached, cut into 8 wedges

1 small red bell pepper, seeded, deribbed, and finely diced

1 cup [240 ml] apple cider vinegar

¼ cup [50 g] sugar

1 tsp minced garlic

Made with a very flavorful broth, enriched with the natural sweetness of cabbage, this dish is 98 percent Pennsylvania Dutch. The 2 percent that I bring to the table is cooking off the liquid at the end, which allows the cabbage to char and the salty, vinegary spice mix to really pop.

SERVES 4 TO 8   In a bowl, combine 6 Tbsp [85 g] of the butter, the vinegar, 2 Tbsp of the salt, the peppercorns, bay leaf, and baking soda. Add to a Dutch oven or large pot, and fill the pot halfway up with cold water. Cover, and bring to a boil over high heat. Lower the heat to medium and simmer for 30 minutes. After 30 minutes, add the cabbage wedges. Cover and let cook for 10 to 15 minutes or until the cabbage is tender.

Carefully pour as much of the water out of the pot as you can. Return the pot to the heat and continue cooking over low heat until all the moisture is gone, about 5 minutes.

Add the bell pepper, vinegar, sugar, and garlic to the pot, along with the remaining 1 Tbsp of salt and 6 Tbsp [85 g] of butter. Turn the heat to high, and gently combine the cabbage with the vinegar and fat mixture until evenly coated. Serve immediately.

HOT-PEPPER SAUCE WATERMELON SALAD

1 large seedless watermelon, rinds removed and flesh cubed

2 red onions, thinly sliced

3 seedless hothouse cucumbers, diced

½ bunch fresh parsley, stemmed and finely chopped

1 cup [240 ml] apple cider vinegar

1 cup [240 ml] olive oil

½ cup [120 ml] hot-pepper sauce

6 Tbsp [90 g] sugar

¼ cup [60 ml] fresh lime juice

4 tsp kosher salt

2 tsp Dijon mustard

There's a myth about Black folks that they walk around with bottles of hot sauce in their bags. Well, in my mother's case, this happens to have been true. Whenever she went out to eat, be it at a diner or a three diamond hotel resort, the food was never tasty or spicy enough for her. Cue her personal hot sauce stash.

As for Nana, one of her (many) personal culinary obsessions was fruit. She'd always keep a big ole bowl of diced watermelon in the fridge during the summer, and whatever we didn't demolish during the day would inevitably find its way to the dinner table at night.

You can probably guess where I'm going with the inspiration for this salad: My mom would always splash hot sauce all over Nana's watermelon. And I've got to give it up to her, because she knew exactly what she was doing.

SERVES 10 TO 12   Combine the watermelon, onions, cucumbers, and parsley in a large mixing bowl. Store in the refrigerator until ready to use.

In a blender, combine the apple cider vinegar, olive oil, hot-pepper sauce, sugar, lime juice, salt, and Dijon mustard and blend until smooth. Toss the watermelon salad with the dressing. Cover and refrigerate for 2 hours before serving.

GREEN LEAF LETTUCE AND CORNBREAD PANZANELLA

FOR THE CORNBREAD TOPPING

2 cups [455 g] dry or stale cornbread cubes (you can use Nana's Cornbread recipe on page 205 or store-bought cornbread)

2 Tbsp butter

¼ cup [25 g] whole oats

¼ cup [40 g] flaxseeds

1 cup [85 g] nutritional yeast

¼ cup [30 g] crumbled pecans

2 Tbsp fresh thyme leaves

FOR THE PANZANELLA

8 baby yellow pattypan squash, halved

2 Tbsp olive oil

Kosher salt and freshly cracked black pepper

1 head green leaf lettuce, quartered

1 cup [240 ml] Buttermilk Ranch Dressing (page 89) or your favorite store-bought dressing

10 ripe cherry tomatoes, halved

½ red onion, thinly sliced

½ lb [230 g] green beans, halved, blanched, and shocked (see sidebar, page 100)

5 red radishes, thinly sliced

As with so many other things, Nana had a million ways to use up leftover cornbread. There was always some form of cornbread stuffing in the oven, and day-old chunks would find their way into the bottom of bowls for soups or stews. My cornbread topping adds a terrific texture to pretty much any salad or vegetable-based dish, so you'll be happy to have plenty of this left over too!

To dry out fresh cornbread, cut into small cubes and let sit uncovered for a day on a baking sheet. Then pop in a 375°F [190°C] oven for 20 minutes, and store in an airtight container on the counter for up to 7 days.

SERVES 4   *To make the cornbread topping:* Put the dried cornbread in a food processor and pulse until you get fine crumbs. In a sauté pan over low heat, add the butter and the cornbread crumbs. Cook, stirring occasionally, until the crumbs are nicely toasted, about 3 minutes. Add the oats and flaxseeds and continue to stir for 5 minutes more. Remove from the heat and add the nutritional yeast, pecans, and thyme. Let cool to room temperature.

cont'd

To make the panzanella: Preheat the oven to 375°F [190°C]. In a bowl, drizzle the squash with the olive oil, rubbing to ensure even coating on all sides, and season with salt and pepper. Spread on a baking sheet, cut-side down, and roast for 20 minutes.

Meanwhile, place a lettuce quarter on each plate, and drizzle each with about 2 Tbsp of Buttermilk Ranch Dressing.

In a mixing bowl, combine the cherry tomatoes, onions, green beans, radishes, and the roasted squash and toss with the remaining dressing, or as much as needed to just coat. Evenly distribute the vegetables atop the lettuce wedges. Sprinkle with the cornbread topping and serve.

HOW TO BLANCH
AND SHOCK VEGETABLES

You always want the "shock" water (ice water bath) to have the same flavor as the "blanching" water (the boiling water used to blanch your vegetables). So if the blanching water is salted, then the shock water also needs to be salted. This way, you don't rinse away all the flavor through the shock process. Also, when blanching the beans, trim off only the stem tip. Trimming both ends lets hot liquid pass through the beans and make them soggy. If you want the beans cut into shorter lengths, trim the stem tip, blanch and shock the whole beans, then cut to desired lengths.

IN NANA'S GARDEN

Nana was the first farm-to-table cook I knew. She cultivated a flourishing backyard landscape of flowers, plants, fruits, and vegetables, all destined to eventually make their way into our kitchen. And she was as instinctive a gardener as she was a cook. She knew when to prune and when to pick, saying that just because something looked ripe didn't mean it was ready. When pain in her ankle or hand joints would flare up, she'd proclaim it meant rain or bad weather was coming. She would plant certain crops downwind from others, knowing that the ladybugs and other helpful garden critters would respond well to the placement.

These amateur farming skills, probably taught to her by her own older generations, went deeper than just putting a seed in the ground. She paid attention throughout the process, studying how everything grew, with a mind to how they'd eventually taste on a plate. And the attention she lavished on her plants directly mirrored the way she tended to her family. She was there through every stage, alternately providing nourishment, care, and even a bit of tough love when needed, always with an eye on the endgame.

CHARRED RADICCHIO SALAD
WITH COLA-BOILED PEANUTS AND AMISH CHEDDAR

FOR THE GREENS

2 heads radicchio

¼ cup [60 ml] olive oil

Kosher salt and freshly
cracked black pepper

1 large head frisée lettuce,
leaves separated

FOR THE GRAPES

1 lb [455 g] large red seedless
grapes, washed and thinly
sliced into rings

2 Tbsp olive oil or blended oil

3 Tbsp chopped fresh
oregano

2 tsp kosher salt

2 tsp sugar

2 tsp freshly cracked black
pepper

FOR THE PEANUTS

4 cups [960 ml] Coca-Cola

2 cups [280 g] shelled raw
peanuts

2 Tbsp Old Bay seasoning

2 tsp kosher salt

FOR THE LEMON SUMAC DRESSING

3 Tbsp ground sumac

½ cup [120 ml] mayonnaise

Juice of 1 lemon

2 Tbsp apple cider vinegar

½ tsp kosher salt

Amish Cheddar (or sharp
Cheddar) cheese, for serving

An outdoor grill is ideal for cooking lettuce, since you'll get great char and smokiness, although a stove top also works in a pinch. And while I can't resist showering the top of this salad with the farm-made Amish Cheddar I grew up with, any salty, well-aged cheese will do.

SERVES 6   *To make the greens:* Cut the radicchio heads in half, leaving the stem so the leaves stay together. Rub with the olive oil and sprinkle with salt and pepper to coat.

If using a grill, preheat to medium-high. Place the radicchio cut-side down on the grill and let it char. Once you get nice blackened color on the cut side, about 2 minutes, flip and repeat on the other sides. Move to a cooler side of the grill, letting the residual heat wilt the radicchio to make it tender, about 5 minutes.

If you don't have a grill, preheat the oven to 300°F [150°C]. Heat a cast-iron pan over medium-high heat and char the radicchio on all sides. Make sure to have the exhaust fan on, as your kitchen may get a little smoky. Once you've achieved a good char, transfer the pan to the oven and cook until the radicchio is halfway wilted and tender, about 5 minutes.

Once tender, let the radicchio cool, then cut into bite-size squares for the salad. Mix with the frisée and set aside.

To make the grapes: Preheat the oven to 350°F [180°C]. Put the sliced grapes in a stainless steel bowl. Add the olive oil, oregano, kosher salt, sugar, and black pepper and toss until coated. Spread the grapes out on a baking sheet and roast in the oven for 20 minutes. Remove and let cool to room temperature. Set aside.

To make the peanuts: Add the Coca-Cola, peanuts, Old Bay seasoning, and kosher salt to a small saucepan, and bring to a hard simmer over medium-high heat, cooking for 30 minutes or until the liquid thickens slightly. Drain the peanuts from the syrup and let cool on a small baking sheet. Set aside.

To make the dressing: Mix the sumac with 3 Tbsp of hot water in a small bowl. Let sit for about 5 minutes. In a blender, combine the sumac water with the mayonnaise, lemon juice, apple cider vinegar, salt, and an additional ¼ cup [60 ml] of water, and process until fully incorporated. You can store any leftover dressing in an airtight container for up to 1 week.

To make the salad: In a mixing bowl, combine the radicchio and frisée mixture with just enough dressing to coat. Lay the dressed greens on a plate. Scatter with some of the roasted grapes and the peanuts, and finish with shaved Cheddar on top. Serve immediately.

RED BEAN PORRIDGE

2 Tbsp red palm oil
or olive oil

2 small chicken livers

3 garlic cloves, minced

1 onion, finely diced

1 green bell pepper, seeded,
deribbed, and finely diced

1 Fresno chile, seeded and
minced (optional)

2 cups [320 g] dried red
kidney beans, soaked
overnight

6 cups [1.4 L] chicken broth

1 cup [100 g] whole oats,
toasted

1 cup [180 g] cooked
Carolina Gold rice

Kosher salt and freshly
cracked black pepper

Crispy shallots, for serving
(optional)

This is a dish to prepare when you ain't got nothing in the pantry, but you got lots of mouths to feed. I remember enjoying this porridge plenty of times as a child, not realizing that we were on the verge of being out on the street, and that this could have been our last meal for days. I've prettified my version a bit with vibrantly colored beans and a few standout ingredients like red palm oil, a smoky staple of West African cuisine. But it's as stick-to-your-ribs and simple as it ever was. *Note:* Soaking the beans overnight really shortens the cooking time.

SERVES 10   In a large Dutch oven or heavy-bottomed pot over medium-high heat, melt the red palm oil. Add the chicken livers, crushing with a spoon while cooking, and cook until well done, about 8 minutes.

Add the garlic, onions, bell pepper, and Fresno chile and continue to cook over medium-high heat until caramelized, about 4 minutes. Drain the soaked red beans and add them to the pot along with the chicken broth. Bring to a boil, then lower the heat to medium and let simmer for 40 to 50 minutes, or until the beans are tender and beginning to fall apart.

Add the oats and cooked rice and lower the heat to medium-low. Cook, stirring, until the mixture begins to thicken, 5 to 8 minutes. Season with salt and pepper and continue to simmer for 10 minutes. Turn off the heat and portion into small bowls. Top with crispy shallots, if desired, and serve.

PICKLED COLLARD "RIBS" AND BEANS

¼ cup [60 ml] blended oil (half vegetable or canola oil, half olive oil)

1 bunch collard greens, stems cut into 1 in [2.5 cm] pieces, leaves cut into thin ribbons

1 large red onion, halved and thinly sliced

1 red bell pepper, seeded, deribbed, and thinly sliced

1 yellow bell pepper, seeded, deribbed, and thinly sliced

3 garlic cloves, minced

1 Tbsp Urfa biber chili powder

½ tsp ground allspice

½ cup [120 ml] vegetable stock

One 15 oz [430 g] can white beans, rinsed and drained

¼ cup [35 g] jerk seasoning

¼ cup [60 ml] apple cider vinegar

1 Tbsp sugar

I've always wanted to create an all-rib menu, albeit one that doesn't include your traditional pork or beef ribs. Instead, it would include things like hamachi or swordfish collars, ribs from plants such as collards, and vanilla bean "ribs" made into dessert. I'm telling you, this rib menu would be next level, and had I made it to the final two on *Top Chef*, it's what I would have made. I'm confident it would have blown the socks off of the judges, and I'm hoping this dish does the same to you.

These collard ribs are great as part of an entirely vegetarian take on a traditional Southern dinner when served with Chicken-Fried Tempeh (page 115).

SERVES 6 In a Dutch oven or heavy-bottomed pot, heat the oil over medium-high heat. Add the collard stems and stir frequently until they are crisp-tender, about 4 minutes. Add the onions, peppers, garlic, chili powder, and allspice, and continue to cook, stirring, until the onions and peppers are translucent and the spices are fragrant, about 3 minutes.

Add the vegetable stock and cover the pot. Cook for 3 to 5 minutes or until the collard stems are completely tender. Add the collard leaves, white beans, jerk seasoning, vinegar, and sugar. Cook, stirring, until the collard leaves are wilted, about 3 minutes.

You can serve this as a side dish or use as a base for Chicken-Fried Tempeh (page 115) or any protein of your choice.

CAULIFLOWER RICE AND BEANS

1 large head cauliflower

2 Tbsp butter

¼ cup [60 ml] blended oil
(half vegetable or canola oil,
and half olive oil)

½ onion, finely diced

4 garlic cloves, minced

1 bunch lacinato kale,
stemmed and cut into ribbons

3 Tbsp Cajun or blackening
seasoning

1 Tbsp sugar

1 tsp liquid smoke

1 cup [160 g] canned pinto
beans, rinsed and drained

Kosher salt

I'm not generally big on food trends. They're sort of the equivalent of one long chain letter among chefs. But loving rice as I do, I make an exception for cauliflower rice; it would be a shame if it couldn't be enjoyed by everyone (including those sensitive to rice). Cauliflower is an excellent stand-in for my favorite grain and, paired with beans, serves as a health-conscious take on a dish beloved by so many cultures.

SERVES 4 Trim the leaves off the cauliflower and shred the florets and stems on a box grater. You can use a food processor if you intend to cook the cauliflower right away, but if you let it sit too long, it will get gray and watery.

Heat a cast-iron pan over high heat and add the butter and oil. When sizzling, add the cauliflower, onion, and garlic, and stir frequently until translucent, about 4 minutes.

Add the kale, Cajun seasoning, sugar, and liquid smoke and continue to cook, stirring frequently, until the kale begins to wilt, about 5 minutes. Add the beans and stir until everything is hot. Season with salt and serve immediately.

AMISH BAKED BEANS

1 lb [455 g] dried pinto beans

1 lb [455 g] ground beef

½ lb [240 g] fatback, diced (or bacon, for a total of 1 lb [455 g])

½ lb [240 g] bacon, diced

1 smoked pork neck bone

1 cup [140 g] diced onion

1 cup [120 g] diced green bell pepper

3 cups [720 ml] beef broth

1½ cups [300 g] packed brown sugar

One 15 oz [430 g] can tomato paste

One 15 oz [430 g] can tomato sauce

½ cup [160 g] molasses

½ cup [120 ml] ketchup

3 Tbsp Worcestershire sauce

2 Tbsp Dijon mustard

1 Tbsp Louisiana-style hot sauce

2 tsp liquid smoke

1 tsp garlic powder

Kosher salt and freshly cracked black pepper

Why use dried beans when you can just open a few cans of beans instead? Besides being worlds tastier, dried beans go a long way—1 lb [455 g] yields almost three times as much cooked. Soaking beans overnight is best, but in case you forget (which happens quite a bit in professional kitchens), letting them sit for 2 hours in hot water is a viable shortcut. Incidentally, Nana would always take her bean-soaking liquid and water the plants with it. Like I said, she wasted nothing.

SERVES 8 Sort the dried beans, discarding any stones or discolored beans. Place the beans in a large pot or bowl and fill with enough water to cover the beans by 3 in [7.5 cm]. Soak for 24 hours.

After 24 hours, drain the beans, put them in a pot, and cover by 3 in [7.5 cm] of cold water. Bring to a boil over high heat. Lower to a simmer and cook the beans until they're tender but still have some bite, about 1 hour. Drain the beans and set aside.

Preheat the oven to 300°F [150°C].

In a skillet, sauté the ground beef over medium heat until cooked through and brown, about 8 minutes. Drain off any liquid and add the beef to a large baking dish. Clean the excess fat from the pan and add the fatback (if using). Cook until it just begins to color and render its fat, about 4 minutes. Drain off any liquid and add the fatback to the baking dish. Clean the excess fat from the pan and add the bacon. Cook until it just begins to color and render its fat, about 4 minutes. Add the bacon to the baking dish, along with its rendered fat.

Add the drained beans to the baking dish, along with the pork neck bone, onion, bell pepper, broth, brown sugar, tomato paste, tomato sauce, molasses, ¼ cup [60 ml] of the ketchup, Worchestershire, mustard, hot sauce, liquid smoke, and garlic powder. Stir well to combine. Cover the dish tightly with aluminum foil and bake for 3 hours.

Remove the foil and stir in the remaining ¼ cup [60 ml] of ketchup. Season with salt and pepper. Return the uncovered baking dish to the oven and bake for 2 hours more, or until tender. Serve hot.

HAM HOCK AND BEAN TERRINE

5 lb [2.3 kg] cooked smoked ham hocks

4 cups [960 ml] chicken or pork broth

2 sprigs fresh rosemary, leaves picked and finely chopped

2 fresh bay leaves

1 tsp ground coriander

2 tsp freshly cracked black pepper

1 head garlic

One 15 oz [430 g] can white beans, drained and rinsed

3 Tbsp chopped fresh parsley

2 tsp fresh lemon juice

2 tsp kosher salt

5 gelatin sheets

1 Tbsp olive oil

1 onion, finely diced

2 celery stalks, finely diced

2 carrots, peeled and finely diced

The French may be celebrated for their charcuterie, but I think the Pennsylvania Dutch give them a real run for their money. Like my Southern ancestors, the Pennsylvania Dutch are artists when it comes to making something from nothing, such as a beautiful charcuterie board out of mere scraps. This is evidenced by scrapple, of course, but also Lebanon bologna, kielbasa, seimaaga (pig's stomach), souse, and ham loaves, which serve as direct inspiration for this bean-studded terrine. Paired with chow-chow, it's worthy of gracing the tables of any Parisian bistro—or Amish soul food kitchen! *Note:* You'll need to start this at least a day in advance.

MAKES ONE 2 BY 11 BY 3 IN [5 BY 28 BY 7.5 CM] TERRINE Put the ham hocks, broth, rosemary, bay leaves, coriander, and 1 tsp of the black pepper in a medium saucepan over high heat. Bring to a boil, then lower to a medium-low simmer. Cover and cook for 1 hour.

Strain the stock into a pot or container. Discard the herbs and pick the meat off the bones, discarding excess fat and skin. Coarsely chop the meat and set aside. Reserve 2 cups of the stock and keep warm. Any remaining stock can be cooled and stored in the freezer in airtight containers.

Preheat the oven to 400°F [200°C].

cont'd

Peel away the papery outermost layer of the garlic head and cut ¼ in [6 mm] off the top of the head to just expose the cloves. Wrap in aluminum foil and roast in the oven for 45 minutes. Set aside until cool enough to handle, then push the cloves out of their papery wrapping into a bowl and mash with a fork. Add the beans, parsley, lemon juice, salt, and the remaining 1 tsp of pepper and stir to combine.

"Bloom" the gelatin sheets by placing in a bowl of cold water for 10 minutes. After 10 minutes, squeeze out any excess water from the sheets. The gelatin will be goopy. Add the gelatin to the warm stock and whisk or blend with a stick blender until completely dissolved.

Add the olive oil to a skillet over medium-high heat. Add the onion, celery, and carrot and sauté until translucent and tender, about 5 minutes. Turn off the heat, add the white bean mixture, stir to combine, and set aside.

Line a terrine mold or loaf pan with plastic wrap, letting at least 2 in [5 cm] of excess hang over the edges. Make alternating layers of the chopped ham hocks and white bean mixture, lightly packing down each layer. Pour the warm stock-gelatin mixture over the top, tapping the mold gently to make sure the liquid seeps into all the nooks and crannies. Fold the excess plastic wrap over the top to cover.

Cut a piece of cardboard to fit snugly over the top of the terrine mold. Top with weights such as cans or plates and refrigerate for 24 hours.

After 24 hours, remove the weights and cardboard and invert the terrine over a plate. Remove the plastic and cut the terrine into ½ in [12 mm] slices. Serve with salad greens and mustard or the chow-chow of your choice.

CHICKEN-FRIED TEMPEH

One 8 oz [226 g] package store-bought tempeh

1 cup [140 g] all-purpose flour

1 tsp kosher salt

1 tsp freshly cracked black pepper

1 tsp garlic powder

½ tsp cayenne pepper

3 eggs, beaten

½ cup [120 ml] vegetable or canola oil

How does soybean-based tempeh jibe with Amish soul food culture? Making tempeh involves the centuries-old human practice of fermentation (some of the first yogurt was produced in goat bags in the heat of North Africa), so I'd say it fits in just as well as anywhere. I especially love battering blocks of tempeh and serving it up chicken-fried style over Pickled Collard "Ribs" and Beans (page 107). It's a truly modern version of a deeply soulful meal.

SERVES 2   Cut the tempeh in half widthwise to form two thin rectangles. In a dish, combine the flour, salt, pepper, garlic powder, and cayenne. Evenly dip the two tempeh rectangles into the beaten egg and then coat with the flour mixture.

Add the oil to a frying pan and heat over medium heat to 350°F [180°C]. Add the tempeh and fry until golden brown and crispy, about 2 minutes per side. Transfer the tempeh to paper towels to drain.

Serve the tempeh atop Pickled Collard "Ribs" and Beans or your favorite chow-chow.

CRISPY YUCCA WITH SUMAC AND LEMON

4 tsp kosher salt

2 tsp sugar

2 tsp ground sumac

2 tsp lemon juice powder
(available online)

1 tsp ground cumin

1 large yucca, peeled, cored,
and cut into 16 wedges

Canola oil, for frying

Also known as cassava or manioc, yucca is a starchy root that can be boiled and mashed into the West African staple called fufu (their stand-in for rice, wheat, and corn). It can also serve as a replacement for potatoes. That was my thought process here. These are essentially turbo-charged french fries, jazzed up with a double bolt of citrus from dark red Middle Eastern sumac and a sprinkle of lemon powder.

SERVES 4   In a small bowl, mix together the salt, sugar, sumac, lemon juice powder, and cumin and set aside. Put the yucca wedges in a saucepan with enough water to cover and boil until just tender, about 30 minutes. Drain and dry on a clean kitchen towel and let cool to room temperature.

Fill a cast-iron pan or Dutch oven a third of the way up with canola oil. Heat the oil to 350°F [180°C]. Working in batches, add a few pieces of yucca at a time and fry until golden brown all over, about 5 minutes. Using a slotted spoon, transfer the yucca from the oil to a stainless steel bowl and liberally sprinkle with the seasoning mixture. Serve while hot as a side dish.

PENNSYLVANIA DUTCH TATER TOT CASSEROLE

FOR THE TATER TOTS

2 lb [910 g] russet potatoes

1 yellow onion, peeled, one end cut off

2 Tbsp potato starch

Kosher salt and freshly cracked black pepper

Alternatively, you can use a 28 oz [793 g] package of store-bought baked tots

Vegetable oil, for frying

FOR THE SHORT RIBS

3 Tbsp vegetable oil

2 lb [910 g] boneless beef short ribs, cut into ½ in [12 mm] pieces, or ground beef

2 Tbsp all-purpose flour

2 tsp kosher salt

2 cups [280 g] diced onion

1 cup [120 g] diced celery

1 cup [140 g] diced carrot

One 15 oz [430 g] can diced tomato

2 garlic cloves, peeled and minced

FOR THE CHEESE SAUCE

6 Tbsp [85 g] butter

6 Tbsp [60 g] all-purpose flour

3 cups [720 ml] milk

3 oz [85 g] shredded Cheddar cheese

1 oz [30 g] grated Parmesan cheese

3 cups [680 g] shredded Gruyère cheese

Buttermilk Ranch Dressing (page 89), for serving (optional)

Tater tots were a favorite of mine as a kid, and even as the years went by, these crunchy potato bites still spoke to me. I realized that during all those childhood years of eating tots atop casseroles, I was paying attention to only the perfect, golden exterior, without a bit of appreciation for what was going on within. In this way, these potato nuggets can serve as an analogy for life: Revisiting this dish underlined my realization that anyone can make the surface look good, but the real value lies in what's happening inside.

SERVES 6   Preheat the oven to 325°F [165°C].

To make the tots: Add the potatoes to a large pot of water and bring to a boil over high heat. Boil for 15 minutes, then drain and let cool completely.

cont'd

Once cooled, grate the potatoes and the onion into a large stainless steel bowl, using the medium holes of a box grater. Add the potato starch, season with salt and pepper, and stir to combine. The mixture should be dry, so pour off any extra liquid. Form into 1 oz [30 g] tater tots.

Add the oil to a Dutch oven or heavy-bottomed pan and heat to 350°F [180°C]. Line a plate with paper towels. In batches, add the tots and cook, turning occasionally with a slotted spoon, until evenly golden brown and crispy. Transfer to the paper towel–lined plate and set aside. Alternatively, cook store-bought tater tots according to the package directions.

To make the short ribs: Discard the used oil from the pan, give the pan a quick wipe, and add the 3 Tbsp of fresh oil to the pan. Heat over medium-high heat.

Toss the beef with the flour and salt until evenly coated. Add to the pan, working in batches if needed, and sear, turning occasionally, until brown on all sides, 7 to 10 minutes. Transfer the seared meat to a baking dish and arrange in a single layer.

If using ground beef, heat the oil as directed and cook the beef (skipping the flour coating) until just browned through, about 5 minutes. Render away all but 1 Tbsp of fat before adding to the baking dish.

Add the onion, celery, and carrot to the pan and cook over medium heat for 10 minutes, or until they begin to brown. Add the tomatoes and garlic, turn down the heat to medium-low, and cook for 10 minutes more. Pour the mixture over the meat in the baking dish and spread in an even layer.

Preheat the oven to 325°F [165°C].

To make the cheese sauce: In a saucepan, melt the butter over medium-high heat. Add the flour and whisk to combine. Lower the heat to medium and slowly add the milk, whisking all the while, and bring the mixture to a simmer, stirring regularly so the bottom doesn't scorch. Once it comes to a simmer, remove from the heat and whisk in the Cheddar and Parmesan until fully combined and smooth.

Pour the cheese sauce in an even layer over the vegetables. Top with an even layer of the Gruyère. Arrange the tater tots in rows over the top, until it's completely covered.

Bake the casserole for 40 minutes, or until the inside is hot and gooey. Serve as is or drizzled with Buttermilk Ranch Dressing.

THE ALL-AMERICAN TATER TOT

To me, tater tots scream Americana, and, as a kid, eating them always made me feel like I was part of something. The rare instances I got to eat at a friend's house, tots would invariably be on their dinner table. Sometimes they'd even show up at our home too, which was nice, because they didn't directly speak to our African American background. In my mind, tater tots spoke to white folks. They reminded me of all the TV commercials in the mid-1980s, where white families would come together and have dinner at the same table with the mother and the father (which I didn't have).

In the 1980s, young Black men under the age of eighteen were considered an endangered species. Because of suicide, homicide, drugs, and Black-on-Black crime, many young Black men never saw their twenty-first birthdays. When the evening news came on, there was story after story about the negative effects of this new music called rap, which all my friends were listening to, and my people being beaten up, cuffed up, and locked up. Not a day went by where I didn't feel some element of shame for my own race, knowing that, although that wasn't me, that's probably how America looked at me as I entered a store or walked down the street.

Even then, it was food that took me to a different place. It may sound silly, but tater tots made me feel like the boy in those commercials, a part of safe America, eating what everyone else ate.

LOW COUNTRY POTATO SALAD

2 lb [910 g] waxy potatoes, such as Red Bliss

4 eggs, hard-boiled, peeled, and diced

½ cup [120 g] mayonnaise

½ cup [130 g] sweet relish

½ cup [70 g] finely diced red onion

3 Tbsp yellow mustard

2 Tbsp finely minced fresh parsley

2 Tbsp pickle juice

2 tsp onion powder

2 tsp kosher salt

1 tsp freshly cracked black pepper

1 tsp garlic powder

1 Tbsp paprika

You may have seen the playful memes of folks putting raisins in the potato salad. That will certainly get your Black card revoked, and you'll find yourself invited to fewer family gatherings.

As a professional chef, I've made potato salad in many ways. But whatever you add, these are the ingredients you can't subtract: mayo, mustard, relish (or some sweet pickled component), hard-boiled eggs, and paprika. As long as you retain those core elements, you can ad lib any way you please.

SERVES 8   In a medium saucepan over high heat, submerge the potatoes in enough water to cover and boil, uncovered, until they are fork-tender, about 45 minutes. Drain and let cool completely so they don't get gummy. Once cool, dice the potatoes and place them in a mixing bowl. Add the eggs, mayonnaise, sweet relish, onion, mustard, parsley, pickle juice, onion powder, salt, pepper, and garlic powder and fold together until well combined. Cover and refrigerate until cold, at least 1 hour. Sprinkle with paprika and serve.

BUCKWHEAT AND ROASTED CARROTS WITH MUSHROOMS

FOR THE ROASTED CARROTS

1 bunch baby carrots with tops

1 small handful frisée greens

Juice of 1 lemon, plus more for serving

3 Tbsp olive oil

2 tsp kosher salt

1 tsp ground cumin

1 tsp ground allspice

1 tsp ground ginger

FOR THE BUCKWHEAT AND MUSHROOMS

3 Tbsp butter

2 Tbsp olive oil

2 shallots, thinly sliced

2 oz [55 g] oyster mushrooms, trimmed and cleaned

1 Tbsp finely chopped fresh thyme leaves

Kosher salt and freshly cracked black pepper

1 cup [180 g] buckwheat groats, cooked according to package directions

Yam Molasses (page 46), for serving

I like to use small, skin-on carrots (not those machine-cut stubs), as they're sweeter when roasted. Choose mushrooms with a deeply earthy flavor, such as oyster mushrooms, that can really take a hard grilling or sear and still stay in one piece.

SERVES 4 TO 6   Preheat the oven to 350°F [180°C].

To make the roasted carrots: Cut off the carrot tops and cut one-third of the tops into 1 in [2.5 cm] pieces (save or discard the rest). Toss the chopped tops with the frisée greens and dress with the lemon juice and 1 Tbsp of the olive oil. Refrigerate until ready to use.

Place the whole baby carrots in a bowl and toss with the remaining 2 Tbsp of olive oil along with the kosher salt, cumin, allspice, and ginger. Place on a baking sheet in a single layer and roast for 25 minutes, or until tender. Remove from the oven and let cool to room temperature on the baking sheet.

To make the buckwheat and mushrooms: In a cast-iron skillet or sauté pan over medium-high heat, melt the butter with the olive oil. Add the shallots and cook, stirring frequently, until translucent, about 3 minutes. Add the mushrooms and thyme and season with salt and pepper. Cook, stirring frequently, until the mushrooms are tender, about 4 minutes. Add the cooked buckwheat, turn the heat to high, and stir continuously for about 6 minutes, until browned and toasted, then transfer to serving plates. Top with the carrots and drizzle with yam molasses and a squeeze of lemon. Top with the carrot top–frisée salad.

MUSTARD GREENS AND LEMONGRASS FRIED RICE

¼ cup blended oil (such as half vegetable or canola oil, half olive oil)

6 garlic cloves, minced

¼ stalk lemongrass, minced

½ pound [230 g] pancetta, finely diced (optional)

3 cups [540 g] cooked Carolina Gold rice

1 lb [455 g] mustard greens, stems cut into small pieces, leaves cut into larger pieces

2 Tbsp soy sauce

½ cup [120 ml] chicken or vegetable stock

¼ cup [60 ml] Yam Molasses (page 46) or regular molasses

Kosher salt

3 Tbsp chopped fresh parsley

Our old apartment in Brooklyn was located right above our restaurant. We always had extra cooked rice available in our multicultural home upstairs and an abundance of greens in our Amish soul food establishment downstairs, so the idea for this dish sprang up pretty seamlessly.

SERVES 6   In a cast-iron or heavy-bottomed skillet, heat the oil over medium heat. Add the garlic and lemongrass and cook until fragrant, about 1 minute. Add the pancetta and cook until caramelized, about 3 minutes.

Add the rice and cook, stirring frequently, until toasted and fragrant, about 4 minutes. Add the mustard greens, soy sauce, stock, and molasses. Cook, stirring, until the greens are wilted, about 4 minutes. Season with salt. Remove from the heat, stir in the parsley, and serve.

MY GLOBAL PANTRY

Lemongrass. Pancetta. Sazón Goya. Sumac. Not only has my cooking style been informed by my forebears, but it's also been shaped by friends from various cultures who've welcomed me into their kitchens over the years. For example, one of my mentors was Chef Albert Paris, who (despite his name) exposed me to Italian culinary traditions, like the Feast of the Seven Fishes during Christmastime, and the importance of ricotta pie and lamb on Easter. But more significantly, he helped drive home the early life lesson imparted to me by Nana: that food is connective. It's what brings us together around a table. It's what engages us in conversation, which becomes one of the primary ways we learn about one another. These connections are the very reason that we cook.

Then there's my wife, who is Korean. As with Chef Paris, exposure to her culture has given me valuable insight into all manner of ingredients and techniques, from the fermentation of various styles of kimchi, to the braising of exotic-to-me vegetables such as burdock root, lotus, and genyip. But again, the lessons imparted through conversations with her family have proven just as influential as the lessons I've learned through their cooking. They're reminiscent of what I learned from my family. And they're a reminder that inspiration can be found anywhere and everywhere.

MILLET AND SUMMER CORN

5 cups [1.2 L] chicken stock

4 cups [960 ml] milk

1 cup [160 g] fresh corn, cut off the cob

½ cup [90 g] raw millet

4 Tbsp [55 g] unsalted butter

Kosher salt

This side dish was inspired by my visits to the Snug Harbor Farm on Staten Island. Farmer Jon Wilson and I would just walk the fields and shoot the breeze, discussing family, recipes, and the state of local politics. One day, he was talking about a new strain of corn that he was about to plant, and he asked if I was interested in being one of the first to try it out. It was an heirloom Silver Queen variety that I initially planned to use in risotto, but at the last second, I decided to combine it with millet instead of Arborio rice, while still using the risotto cooking technique. It emerged as a delicious hit that stayed on my restaurant menu all season long.

SERVES 4   In a saucepan over medium-high heat, combine the stock, milk, corn, millet, and butter and bring to a boil. Lower the heat to a simmer, cover the pot, and cook for 20 to 25 minutes, stirring occasionally, until thick and creamy. Season with salt and serve immediately.

SUNSHINE SHERBET DESSERT

2 eggs
1 teaspoon grated lemon rind
½ cup sugar
½ cup light corn syrup
1½ cups light cream
⅛ teaspoon salt
¼ cup lemon juice
¾ cup heavy cream, whipped
2 layers sponge cake
Orange Sauce

Turn refrigerator control to coldest setting. Line a deep 8-inch layer cake pan with foil, allowing it to extend ½ inch up from top. Beat eggs, lemon rind, and sugar together. Blend in corn syrup, light cream, salt, and lemon juice. Pour into freezing tray, and freeze until mushy. Beat with rotary or electric mixer until fluffy. Fold in cream, and pour into foil-lined pan. Put in freezer or refrigerator freezing unit, and freeze until firm. When ready to serve, lift out layer of sherbet, and peel off paper. Put between layers of cake on serving plate. Cut in wedges, and serve with **Orange Sauce:** To make, beat 2 egg yolks, ½ cup sugar, ⅛ teaspoon salt, and juice and grated rind 1 large orange in top part of small double boiler. Cook over simmering water, stirring constantly, until slightly thickened. Cool. Fold in ½ cup heavy cream, whipped. Makes 8 to 10 servings.

MOCHA PUFFS

1 qt. vanilla ice cream
5 tsp. instant coffee
12 small cream puff shells (recipe follows or use a mix)
Chocolate Marshmallow Sauce (recipe follows)

Soften ice cream by putting it in a chilled bowl and mashing with a wooden spoon (work quickly so ice cream doesn't melt). Stir in instant coffee. Put in ice-cube trays or other container and freeze until serving time.

Split cream puff shells and pull out and discard any soft membranes at serving time. Spoon ice cream into shells, replace tops, set on serving plates and spoon hot Chocolate Marshmallow Sauce over. (Serves 6.)

FROZEN EGGNOG PIE

2 cups pretzel crumbs
½ cup melted butter
3 egg yolks, slightly beaten
1 cup sugar
¼ teaspoon salt
½ cup milk
3 tablespoons rum
½ teaspoon nutmeg
3 egg whites
1 cup heavy cream, whipped

Prepare crumbs by crushing pretzels fine in blender or grinder. Mix with butter, and press into buttered 9-inch pie-pan. Chill.

In top part of small double boiler mix egg yolks, ½ cup of the sugar, salt, and milk. Cook over simmering water, stirring constantly, until slightly thickened. Remove from heat, and add rum and nutmeg. Cool. Beat egg whites until almost stiff. Gradually beat in remaining ½ cup sugar. Fold with cream into first mixture. Pile lightly in pie shell, and freeze.

PEACH MARLOW

Makes 6 servings — Woman's Day Kitchen

16 marshmallows (1/4 pound)
1/2 cup peach nectar
1/4 teaspoon almond extract
1/8 teaspoon salt
1 cup undiluted evaporated milk
2 tablespoons lemon juice
Few drops each red and yellow food coloring, if desired

Set refrigerator control for fast freezing. Melt marshmallows in top part of double boiler over boiling water. Add peach nectar, and cook until smooth and blended, stirring constantly. Remove from heat; add extract and salt; cool. Pour evaporated milk into refrigerator tray, and freeze until mushy. Whip until stiff. Add lemon juice. Fold in marshmallow mixture, blending well. Add food coloring to tint a delicate peach color. Put in refrigerator tray, and freeze until firm.

OF DOMESTIC ARTS AND SCIENCES, Inc.

Recipe from:

Serves:

O RABBIT

t oil
d rabbit cut up

beaten
d-half

an iron skillet to about
wash rabbit pieces
running water and pat
er towels. Sprinkle with
per. Make a light batter
ing egg, half-and-half,
and pepper. Dip pieces of
in egg batter to coat, then
d rabbit pieces to the skil-
rown, turning to brown
all sides. Reduce heat and
meat is tender, about 15 to
. Serves 6 to 8.
favorite rabbit recipe was
e by Mehdi-Ziani, the chef-
Mamounia, a Moroccan
t in San Francisco. It is "fin-
n' good" — all the food at
a is — it has to be, for in
and at Mehdi's establish-
eat with your fingers.

OCCAN RABBIT PAPRIKA

3-pound rabbit, cut in

Y.M.C.A.
CAFETERIA
1501 B
25 CENTS
NOT GOOD DETACHED

Y.M.C.A.
CAFETERIA
1501 B
25 CENTS
NOT GOOD DETACHED

Y.M.C.A.
CAFETERIA
1501 B
25 CENTS
NOT GOOD DETACHED

Y.M.C.A.
CAFETERIA
1501 B
25 CENTS
NOT GOOD DETACHED

Y.M.C.A.
CAFETERIA
1501 B
25 CENTS
NOT GOOD DETACHED

foods

siny holiday treat

y season fast
ughts turn to
traditional,
— cookies,
s and holiday

ch as raisins
opular at this
as they are
t commonly-
redients in

t that always
hit is Double
m Pie. Really
under-crust,
t is perfect for
ouse, pot-luck
dinner.
s a delicious
the more
lay pies, such
ncemeat, at
er table.

Crust
am Pie
rust 9-inch pie

4 eggs, slightly beaten
3 tablespoons lemon juice
1½ cups sour cream
1 cup sugar
1 teaspoon vanilla
⅛ teaspoon salt
1 egg yolk
1 tablespoon water
Line pie pan with half of
pastry and sprinkle eve
with raisins. In la
beat together
juice, sou
vanilla an

raisins. Roll out top pastry
very thin. Cover pie, seal and
flute edge.
Beat together egg yolk and
water. Brush surf   pie
with mixtur   1
tables

Jer

fo

What
the holi
"Rhi

Vanishing Oatmeal
raisin cookies
1 cup (2 sticks) margarine
or butter softened
1 cup firmly packed brown
sugar
1 cup granulated sugar
½ eggs
vanilla
ose flour

FARM MADE
APPLE BUTTER
NO SUGAR ADDED
Fresh Apples, Sweet Cider
and Spices.
REFRIGERATE AFTER OPENING
Made by KRESGE FARM FOODS, Inc. ©
Lehighton, Pa. 18235
Net Wt. 19 Oz. (1 Lb. 3 Oz.)

wife's meditation
me as I go about my
Tasks. Give me of
strength, help me to
job so that it may be
and well.

I clean, as I answer the
shop and plan, let me
ence close beside me.
strength and patience.
wisdom and inspiration.
you as I serve the meal

food that I prepare.

IS A FIN...
TE PRO...

DECAL IN U...
RESULTS
ER. IF THER...
EET, CUT APA...
THEN SLIDE DEC...
PRESS OUT ALL...
ALLOW SEVERAL...
COATING WITH C...
(BUT NOT ESS...
LACQUER.
NOTE: (FOR WIND...
TIONS) IF DECALS...
BE SURE TO SP...
DECAL AFTER AP...

SURPRISE
PACKAG...

Bags • Jokes • No...
$1.00 VALUE ONLY...

Windshield deca...
cannot supply...
Box 73, P...

COATESVILLE LODGE
35¢
No. 297

THIS $5.00 COUPON BOOK IS SOLD TO YOU FOR $4.50 — A SAVING OF 10%

Y. M. C. A. CAFETERIA
COATESVILLE, PA.

THIS BOOK SOLD FOR CASH ONLY   No. 1501B

GOOD FOOD IS GOOD HEALTH

Southern Coupon Co., B'ham. Ala., U.S.A.

NTRY O

ONE **VIEW-MASTER** REEL

7 MORE
WONDERS

349
AMISH COUNTRY

VIEW-MASTER
REEL

PENNSYLVANIA
U.S.A

OF THE
WORLD

7 THREE-DIMENSIONAL PICTURES
IN FULL-COLOR KODACHROME

Pennsylvania Dutch Country

KITCHEN
KETTLE
VILLAGE

INTERCOURSE,
PENNSYLVANIA 17534

Cheese
Cheese
Pepper Chutney

PEPPER PARTY PLEASER

salt and pepper. Toss with salad
greens and edible petals.

— Susan Guerrero,
Jennifer Dorazio

¾ cup fresh pineapple chunks or 1
can (8¼ ounces) pineapple chunks,
drained
½ cup seedless red grapes, halved
1 banana, sliced,
½ cup shredded coconut
... a pieces
... slice apples. Place in
... and toss with orange
... oranges, pineapple, grapes,
banana, coconut and pecans. Stir to
mix; cover and chill 30 minutes or
longer. To serve, spoon ambrosia
into stemmed sherbet glasses.
Makes 6 servings.

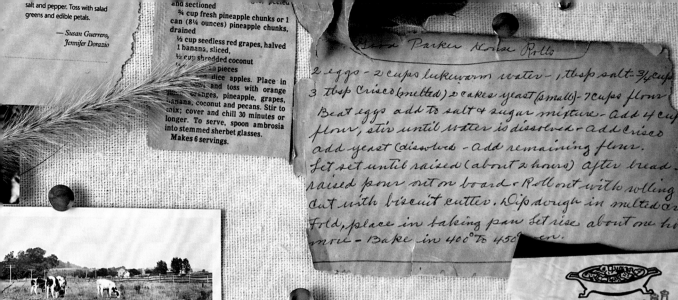

Parker House Rolls

2 eggs - 2 cups lukewarm water - 1 tbsp salt - ¾ cup
3 tbsp Crisco (melted) 2 cakes yeast (small) - 7 cups flour
Beat eggs, add to salt & sugar mixture - Add 4 cup
flour, stir until water is dissolved - Add Crisco
add yeast (dissolved - Add remaining flour.
Let set until raised (about 2 hours) After bread
raised pour out on board - Roll out with rolling pin
cut with biscuit cutter. Dip dough in melted Crisco
Fold, place in baking pan. Let rise about one hour
more - Bake in 400° to 450°

THRIFTY CASSEROLE

4 cups ARNOLD STUFFIN'	2 cups sliced Bermu...
1 cup hot water	1 pound ground beef
1 beef bouillon cube	1 teaspoon salt
6 tablespoons melted butter	¼ teaspoon pepper
1 medium eggplant, peeled & cubed	6 tablespoons Parme...

Add salt and pepper to ground beef. Saute onion, beef a...
in melted butter until beef is browned. Meanwhile melt b...
in hot water and pour over Stuffin'. Mix together with first 3
and spoon into 2 quart casserole. Sprinkle top with Parm...
Bake in preheated oven at 350°F. for about 45 min. Serves...

THE PENNSYLVANIA DUTCH

The early Pennsylvania Dutch settlers were of Swiss and German descent and settled in Eastern Pennsylvania. Today's colorful English speech stems from the translations of their early native tongues. The "Dutch" ancestors left a simple way of life resulting from their discoveries, family amusements, superstitions, folk art and combination of faiths.

❤ EXPRESSIONS

...ssin' wears out . . . cookin' don't • We grow too soon old and
...ate schmart • Levi's tooth ouches him • I've seen him yet al-
...y • My! You look good in the face • Make the door shut •
...w the cow over the fence some hay • Let's walk the street
...n • Poor Jakey . . . he's wonderful sick • I've known
...long already • Ruben makes the grass off • Throw
...down the stairs his hat • Jacob's at the table and
...already • I sit broad, ain't I? • Outen the light

...PERSTITIONS OR "FOLK BELIEFS"

...a house by the same door you entered, or else
...d luck on yourself.

...mstress would hand a need... another seam-
...t; it would bring bad luck...

...shing, don't let a wo...
...catch any fish that d...

...entally put your...
...e a present.

❤ FOLK ART

"Fractur Writing," inspired by the illuminated manuscripts of the middle ages, became a true expression of the Pennsylvania Dutch people. Artistic and functional, this decorative writing has revealed a great deal of vital information about the early settlers.

"Hex Signs" are a decorative design enclosed in a circle and usually painted on barns. These signs were originally thought to have been used to frighten off witches or protect from evil spirits.

With the scarcity of fabric in the early settlement... became quite popular and gave the D... tunity to express her love of form and... terns such as the full-blown tulip and sta...

❤ DISCOVERIES-INVE...

Pretzels along with scrapple. apple but...
at one time only familiar among the P...

The Conestoga Wagon was devel...
speed carrying of excess farm p...
ket in the cities.

...e bi...
HOW A...

...m boll wide...
...m SOON AGAIN

...NDYWINE AS SEEN FROM ROCK RUN ROAD, COATESVILLE, PA.

hours, basting occasionally with pan liquids.

Meanwhile, prepare dressing: tear bread into ½-inch pieces; place in large bowl with onion, celery, parsley, ¾ teaspoon salt, ½ teaspoon pepper, sage and thyme. Mix well and set aside. After 1¼ hours remove roaster from oven. Reserve giblets and drain 2 cups stock into a medium-sized saucepan; hold for gravy. Add water to remaining stock, if necessary, to ...ing to 1½ cups. Ladle into bowl ...dressing mixture; add eggs and ...til thoroughly moistened. ...hands, mold stuffing around ...of roaster to form a "nest." ...ush butter over breast. Return roaster to oven; continue cooking 45 minutes to 1 hour longer or until dressing is cooked and lightly browned and bird-watcher thermometer has popped up.

If desired, serve nested roast from roasting pan. Or run spatula under bird to loosen it and carefully transfer to heated platter, keeping dressing intact. Serve with Creamed Giblet Gravy.

...kes 6 servings.

Creamed Giblet Gravy
...reserved roaster stock
...ved roaster giblets, chopped
...up milk
...cup all-purpose flour
Salt
Pepper

Season with salt and pepper to taste.

Bourbon Sweet Potato Puff
6 medium-sized cooked sweet potatoes or 1 can (40 ounces) sweet potatoes, drained
¼ cup (½ stick) unsalted butter, melted
3 eggs
½ cup firmly packed brownsugar
¾ teaspoon ground cinnamon
¼ teaspoon ground cloves
¼ teaspoon ground nutmeg
2 teaspoons grated orange rind
¼ cup bourbon
1 package (10 ounces) marshmallows

Preheat oven to 350 degrees. Butter a 1½-quart souffle dish or casserole. Peel cooked sweet potatoes. In large bowl, combine

potatoes with remaining ingredients except marshmallows. With electric mixer or food processor, beat or process until fluffy. Turn mixture into prepared dish or casserole; arrange marshmallows over top. Bake 20 minutes or until marshmallows are puffed and golden.

Makes 6 servings.

Stacked Dried-Apple Cake
1½ cups (3 sticks) unsalted butter
2½ cups sugar, divided
4 eggs
3 cups sifted all-purpose flour
1 tablespoon baking powder
1 teaspoon salt
1 cup milk
1½ teaspoons vanilla extract

n connection with a unit on foods, James Adams School pupils learn how to make mud... ...water clear. L. to r. are Emma Corporal (daughter of Carroll C., Safety & Plant Protection... ...Mrs. Hester W. Burton, Cornel Matthews, Raymond Griffey, Rita Haywood and Carmen Brow...

for holiday feasts

...at cream and milk
...zest and leave it for an
...that flavor. Then sugar
...ter are boiled to make a
...There is no
...an boil ...out
...ld ...

baking pan to reach half...
the sides of the pan with fo...
Cover the pan with fo...
place in oven; Bake...
knife inserted in the...
custard comes out...
35 minutes.
Remove baking...
oven and remove...
the pan. Let cool...
minutes, then co...
refrigerate until...
Just before se...
run a knife aroun...
individual p...
me in ...
ards

THIS SPACE FOR WRITING MESSAGES

COATESVILLE, PA
NOV 22
5-PM
1914

U.S. POSTAGE

THIS SPACE FOR ADDRESS ONLY

...pound uncooked)

...cinnamon
...d allspice
...d cloves
... 350 degrees.
... flour 3 8-inch

...h electric mixer
...ream butter and
...fluffy. Add eggs,
...ting after each

... bowl, sift
...ng powder and
...ture to creamed
...g with milk and
...eat on highest
...bout 3 minutes.

...Pour batter into prepared pans and
...ake 20 to 25 minutes. Cakes are
...one when skewer inserted in
...centers comes out clean. Cool 5
...minutes in pans; turn out onto wire
...acks to cool completely.
...In large bowl, combine apples
...emaining ¾ cup sugar, cinnamon,
...lspice and cloves.
...When cakes are cool, split each
...cake horizontally in half to make
...layers. Spread small amount...
...filling over first layer; top w...
...second layer. Spread with filling...
...continue stacking layers and filli...
...cover top and sides of cake...
...apple filling. If desired, prepare...
...day before serving to allow flavors...
...to blend.

ia, pota...

southern

2 tablespoons unsalted butter or
margarine
1 cup chopped onion
2 medium carrots, diced
1 teaspoon crushed marjoram
1 teaspoon crushed thyme leaves
½ teaspoon crushed tarragon
1 teaspoon salt
¼ teaspoon pepper
1 cup light cream
1 bag (16 ounces) Herb Seasoned
Stuffing
½ cup chopped parsley
½ cup chopped walnuts
16- to 18-pound turkey
1 orange
1 lemon
½ cup melted butter or m...
...up honey

... bowl, combine ...
...e juice. Let sta...
...large skillet, brown vea...
...butter, stirring to break
...Add onions and carrots.
...il vegetables are tender;
...Blend in seasonings. Add
...and heat. Remove from heat.
...bowl, combine veal mixture
...rrants and orange juice. Stir
...peridge Farm Herb Seasoned
...ng, parsley and walnuts.
...ff into turkey and truss. Roast
...5 degrees approximately 20 to 25
...utes per pound.
...Meanwhile, grate 1 tablespoon
...ange and lemon peel. Squeeze
...ces and combine with melted
...utter and honey. Use as glaze last
...0 minutes of roasting turkey.
...Makes 16 to 18 servings.

two stuf...

or Chris —
Love you "Muchley"! (smile)

KITCHEN KETTLE VILLAGE
INTERCOURSE, PENNSYLVANIA 17534

KITCHEN KETTLE BLACK RASPBERRY DELIGHT
1 Jar Kitchen Kettle Seedless Black Raspberry Jam
1 lb. softened plain cream cheese
Blend well with medium speed electric mixer.
Great with cookies or animal crackers.

ALL ABOUT FOOD
CLIP 'N' FILE
Tested Recipe Institute

VEGETABLE SAUCES

Combine canned condensed cream of chicken soup with a little mayonnaise and lemon juice; heat. Serve over cooked broccoli.

Combine canned condensed cream of chicken soup ... ½ cup milk. Use ... sauce for scalloped ... toes.

Combine one part peanut butter with two parts milk. Heat and serve over cooked carrots.

No. 12

... a little chopped ...; add canned con-... ed cream of tomato ... and heat. Serve over ... d lima beans. Garnish ... crisp crumbled bacon.

ALL ABOUT FOOD
CLIP 'N' FILE
By Tested Recipe Institute

AMAZING MAYONNAISE

To one cup of mayonnaise add about ¼ cup pineapple juice. Makes a good dressing for a fruit salad.

To a cup of ... add ¼ cup of ... juice. Makes a speedy dressing for tossed salad.

For a cole slaw dressing add a couple of tablespoons of sweet pickle relish to ... cup of mayonnaise.

...-CREAM MENU SAVER

... delicious way to use any ... ftover meat or poultry.

... medium ... Salt
... cooked 2 eggs, beaten
... minced ½ cup chopped
... ons green or ripe olives
leftover 1 tablespoon
... meat, chopped parsley
... allense ... cup sour cream
Buttered bread crumbs

... ned cooked noodles into

... ing as a base. I will repeat the recipe for boiled dressing and then give the method of making cole slaw dressing from it.

§ 26

Boiled Salad Dressing
Two tablespoons cornstarch, 1½ teaspoons dry mustard, 1½ teaspoons salt, one-eighth teaspoon paprika, one-quarter cup granulated sugar, one egg yolk, one-third cup milk, 1½ cups warm milk, one-half cup vinegar.

In a heavy saucepan combine cornstarch, seasonings and sugar and blend well. Add egg yolk beaten well with the one-third cup milk. Add warm milk slowly and then the vinegar, a small amount at a time. Mix well. It will appear curdled before it is completely cooked. Cook over medium heat, stirring constantly, about five minutes after it comes to simmering point. Remove from heat; beat for a few seconds with spoon or egg beater. Let stand until cool. Store in tightly covered jar. If it is too thick when you use it, add a little milk or vinegar to a small amount and mix well.

Cole Slaw Dressing
To one-half cup boiled salad dressing (above) add one teaspoon French mustard, one tablespoon sugar, one teaspoon scraped onion, one tablespoon vinegar, six tablespoons cream.

Griddle Cakes wit ...
Rolls and Butter
French Toas ...
Fried Cornmea ...
Orange ...
Cornmeal ...
Hominy Grits ...
Pearl Barley
Marmalade
Toast
ONE-EGG SALAD DRESSING

---

3 SALAD DRESSINGS
Tomato Dressing

1 package old-fashioned French dressing mix	1½ cups tomato juice ¼ cup each malt vinegar and salad oil

Empty contents of package of mix into a screwtop, quart-size jar. Add remaining ingredients, cover and shake well. Chill. Makes 2 cups.

About 22 calories, 1 gram carbohydrate, no protein and 2 grams fat per tablespoon.

Cooked Salad Dressing

½ teaspoon salt ¼ teaspoon each dry mustard and paprika Dash cayenne 2 tablespoons vinegar	¼ cup nonfat milk 1 egg, beaten ¼ teaspoon non-caloric liquid sweetener

Mix all ingredients in top part of small double boiler. Put over hot water and cook, stirring, until thickened. Cool and chill. Makes ½ cup.

About 13 calories, no carbohydrate, 1 gram protein, 1 gram fat per tablespoon.

Piquant Salad Dressing

½ teaspoon dry mustard Dash monosodium glutamate ¼ teaspoon seasoned salt ½ teaspoon celery salt	1 tablespoon flour ½ cup nonfat milk 1 egg yolk, beaten 3 tablespoons vinegar Few drops non-caloric liquid sweetener

In top part of small double boiler, mix seasonings and flour. Add milk and cook over boiling water, stirring, until thickened. Stir in egg yolk and cook 1 minute longer, stirring. Remove from heat and stir in vinegar and sweetener. Cool; chill. Makes ⅔ cup.

ZUCCHINI [BREAD]

2 LOAVES - 375°   1 HOUR
COOL IN PANS   10 MINUTES

* * * * * * * * * * * * * *

3 EGGS
1 CUP VEGETABLE OIL
1½ CUPS SUGAR
3 MEDIUM SIZE ZUCCHINI GRATED AND DRAINED   (2 cups)
2 TEASPOONS VANILLA
2 CUPS FLOUR (SIFTED)
1/4 TEASPOON BAKING POWDER
2 TEASPOONS BAKING SODA
3 TEASPOONS CINNAMON
1 TEASPOON SALT
1 CUP RAISINS
1 CUP WALNUTS

* * * * * * * * * * * * * *

BEAT EGGS LIGHTLY IN A LARGE BOWL, STIR IN OIL, SUGAR
ZUCCHINI AND VANILLA. SIFT FLOUR, BAKING POWDER
BAKING SODA, CINNAMON AND SALT ONTO WAX PAPER. STIR
INTO EGG MIXTURE UNTIL WELL BLENDED. STIR IN RAISINS,
AND NUTS. SPOON BA[TTER INTO] TWO WELL GREASED 8 x 5 x 3
INCH LOAF PANS. [BAKE UNT]IL CENTER SPRINGS BACK
WHEN LIGHTLY TO[UCHED]

the Pennsylva

♥ Poor Jakey... he's wonderful sick ♥ Late it is already ♥ I've fr

© Malanco

topping, thawed
☐ 1 prepared graham cracker
crust (6 ounces)
☐ 1 cup cold milk
☐ 16-ounce can pumpkin
☐ Two 4-serving size
packages vanilla-flavor
pudding and pie filling
☐ 1 teaspoon ground
cinnamon
☐ ½ teaspoon gr
☐ ¼ teaspoon g

Mix cream chee
sugar in a larg
wire whisk
Gently stir in w
Spread on bottom of gr
cracker crust.

Pour the cold milk int a
large bowl. Add pumpki
pudding mixes and spice
with a wire whisk until
mixed. (Mixture will be t
Spread over cream cheese

Refrigerate 4 hours or u til
set. Garnish with addition
whipped topping, if desire
Store leftover pie in
refrigerator. Makes 8 servings.

Note: You can soften cream
cheese in a microwave oven on
high (100 percent power) for 15
to 20 seconds.

DOUBLE LAYER
CHOCOLATE PIE
☐ 4 ounces cream cheese,
softened
☐ 1 tablespoon milk
☐ 1 tablespoon sugar
☐ 8-ounce tub frozen whipped
topping, thawed
☐ 1 prepared chocolate-flavor

to 20 seconds.

MOCK CRANBERRY
APPLE PIE
☐ 2 cups boiling water
☐ 8-serving size package or
two 4-serving size packages red-
flavor gelatin dessert
☐ ½ cup cold water
☐ ½ teaspoon ground
cinnamon
☐ ½ teaspoon ground cloves
☐ 4 ounces cream cheese,
softened
☐ ¼ cup sugar
☐ ¼ cup frozen whippe
topping, thawed
☐ 1 prepared graham
crumb crust (6 ounces)
☐ 1 medium apple, chopped
☐ ½ cup chopped walnuts
☐ Fresh mint leaves
(optional)

boiling water into gelatin
in a large bowl at least 2
minutes until completely
dissolved. Stir in cold water
and spices. Refrigerate about
1½ hours or until thickened
(spoon drawn through leaves
definite impression).

Meanwhile, mix cream cheese
and sugar in medium bowl with
wire whisk until smooth.
Gently stir in whipped topping.
Spread on bottom of crust.
Refrigerate.

Stir apples and walnuts into
thickened gelatin. Refrigerate
10 to 15 minutes or until
mixture is very thick and will
mound. Spoon over cream
cheese layer.

Roast d in
Sage Dressing
1 Perdue oven stuffer roaster (5 to
7 pounds)
Salt to taste
Pepper to taste
3 cups hot water
1 loaf (1¼ to 1½ pounds) day-old
white bread
1 medium-sized onion, diced
1½ cups diced celery
¼ cup chopped parsley
1½ tablespoons minced fresh sage
or 1¼ teaspoons dried sage
¼ teaspoon dried thyme
2 eggs
1 tablespoon butter or margarine
Creamed Giblet Gravy (recipe
follows)

Preheat oven to 350 degrees.
Remove giblets and rinse roaster
inside and out; pat dry. Sprinkle
inside of bird with salt and pepper.
Tie legs together and fold wings
under. Place roaster in roasting pan
or baking dish along with giblets
Pour in 2 cups hot water. Roast 1¼

Lejay Jewelers
117 GRIFFING AVE.

APPLE
NO SUGAR
Fresh Apples, Sweet
and Spices
REFRIGERATE AFTER OPEN
Made by KRESGE FARM FOODS, Inc. ©
Lehighton, Pa. 18235
Net Wt. 19 Oz. (1 Lb. 3 Oz.)

Soul Food

(From Page E1)

minutes before dinner was to be served.

"We don't have any recipes," Alma said. "My mama never had recipes."

Alma also doesn't measure any of the ingredients. "You just guess and pray it's right," she said.

Alma grew up in Louisiana, one of 15 children. Her mother taught her to cook.

Her daughters are self-proclaimed "women of the '90s." They all work outside of the home. They eat fast food and cook simple dinners for their families.

"We know we get a good, nutritious meal on Sundays," Carol said, winking at her mother.

There's always plenty of food. In fact, the grown children often take home leftovers.

Even when Alma and Carey Sr. are out of town on vacation,

blended. Shape into 1-inch balls; store in airtight container several days
to develop flavor. Roll balls in additional confectioners' sugar before
serving. About 4 dozen cookies.

RUM VARIATION: Substitute 1/2 cup rum for orange juice and orange peel.

Harvest Ham Cakes

Pour small pancakes onto hot griddle. Top each
with 1 tbsp. Underwood Deviled Ham. Cover with
more batter, brown on both sides. Serve with
syrup or with sour cream & hot orange sauce made
by mixing ½ cup of sugar, 1 tbsp. Cornstarch with 1 cup
orange juice. Cook until thickened. Add 3 tbsp. butter.
Serve hot.

MILK SHAKE

1 large very ripe banana
2 tbsp. instant chocolate malted milk
1 cup cold milk
1 scoop vanilla or chocolate ice cream
¼ tsp. vanilla

Peel and break up banana. Whirl in blender or beat with rotary beater until smooth. Add the malted milk powder and a little of the milk and blend well. Add remaining milk, ice cream and vanilla and beat until smooth. Serve in tall glass. (Serves 1.)

MAPLE SODA

2 tbsp. maple syrup
¼ cup light cream
1 scoop maple-flavored ice cream
Ginger ale

Mix maple syrup and cream in a tall glass. Add ice cream and fill glass with ginger ale. (Serves 1.)

½ cup sugar
¼ cup water
1 6-ounce can frozen concentrated orange juice
2 cups buttermilk

Heat sugar and water in a saucepan, stirring until dissolved. Remove from heat and blend in orange juice. Cool. Stir in buttermilk. Pour into a refrigerator tray. Partially freeze (½ to 1 hour), then turn into a bowl and beat until smooth. Return to tray and freeze until firm. Reset control to normal 1 hour before serving. Makes 4 to 6 servings.

P.S. *This makes a tart, smooth sherbet with a decided orange flavor.*

P.P.S. *Ever had buttermilk in sherbet? You'll surely want to try this to see how good it is.*

EGG NOG ICE CREAM
(Lower photo, page 58)

2 eggs
½ cup sugar
Few grains salt
½ teaspoon nutmeg
½ cup corn syrup
1 cup milk
1 cup light cream

Beat eggs until light and lemon-colored. Add sugar, salt, and nutmeg gradually, beating constantly. Blend corn syrup, milk, and cream. Add egg mixture; mix well. Pour into a refrigerator tray. When partially frozen, remove to a bowl and whip

---

LEMON DRINK

½ doz LEMONS
2 Lbs. SUGAR, W.
2 GALS hot WATER
when lukewarm, add 1
cke yeast, keep overnight.
Then add 1 beaten egg
white. Bottle and tie
corks down. May be
used after 24 hours

CHOCOLATE-COFFEE MOUSSE

3 squares unsweetened chocolate
⅓ cup water
¾ cup sugar
⅛ teaspoon salt
3 egg yolks
1 tablespoon instant coffee
1 teaspoon vanilla
2 cups heavy cream, whipped

Turn refrigerator control to coldest setting. Put chocolate and water in saucepan. Bring to boil over low heat, stirring vigorously until blended. Add sugar and salt; simmer 3 minutes, stirring. Gradually stir into well-beaten egg yolks; add coffee, and cool. Fold in vanilla and cream. Pour into refrigerator trays, and freeze until firm. Makes 8 servings.

CHAPTER 4

Hard Times Foods

Pennsylvania Dutch food definitely suffers from underexposure, while Southern fare has recently experienced quite the opposite. Yet it's often misrepresented as a culinary culture built around red velvet cake. Certainly, in the effort to raise Southern cuisine's profile (so it might eventually be regarded with the same esteem as French, Italian, and Japanese fare), Southern chefs have made it a point to put their best foot forward, which is only natural. But that has led to the eager promotion of what's known as "celebration food," which does not necessarily reflect what people regularly eat, or what they ate historically.

I get it: Fried chicken and waffles make a much louder noise than turkey necks and rice. But it's pop music. It's easy, shiny, happy, and everyone enjoys it. But it's not quite in touch with reality. It doesn't dive into the deeper, more truthful, nonprettified story.

Needless to say, times were tough for slaves during the colonial era. They worked the fields for long hours under inhumane conditions and lived every day in fear: of abuse, of sexual assault, of kidnapping, of family separation, and yes, in some cases, of death. And what they cooked and ate largely reflected those conditions and that mentality, which is why it was considered "hard times food."

Hard times food usually consisted of seasonal vegetables and cornbread with some type of flavored broth. Maybe there was salt pork, but otherwise they ate very little meat. And although those foods sound bleak, slaves found a way to make them all delicious and nutritious using techniques and a few ingredients from their African homeland. If you thought that field workers were eating fried chicken on the regular, this was definitely not the case. Their diet revolved around vegetables, beans, and rice and other grains.

I came up in an era where food stamps were a regular thing with the Black folks in my neighborhood. I would stand in the lines with Nana for that big block of government cheese and white bread. When times were particularly hard, she'd have to change her approach in the kitchen. Nana would put cornbread at the bottom of a bowl, for instance, ladle in soup or stew that was mostly collards, peas, or peppers (maybe with some chicken necks for flavor), and that would be your meal. There was always spaetzle too, or a pot of rice on the stove. But a nice steak or good pieces of chicken appeared only rarely, when we could afford them.

Yet somehow the struggle made us stronger. And this is just one of many stories of resilience and triumph in our culture, proving once again that where there's a will, there's a way.

CRISPY FRIED TOMATOES

1 egg

½ cup [120 ml] buttermilk

1 Tbsp hot sauce

½ cup [70 g] all-purpose flour

½ cup [70 g] cornmeal

1 tsp kosher salt

3 large ripe tomatoes, sliced into ¼ in [6 mm] rounds

4 cups [960 ml] canola oil

Sea salt

Fresh lemon juice, for serving

This iconic dish is generally made with green varieties of tomatoes, which have an appealing acidic quality. But keep in mind that there is a difference between a hard, unripe red variety of tomato and a ripe green variety. The latter are the kind that Nana would use in late summer, when we had vine after vine of peak tomatoes at the ready. To be honest, green tomatoes aren't really my bag—I always leaned toward the sweeter red, yellow, or purple varieties. But use whatever you prefer.

This is one of those "keep it simple" recipes. I've had many fried tomatoes in my time, and I'd have to say that at least half aren't executed well. This is because they're too gussied up with crazy breading and overpowering remoulade that makes the tomato second fiddle. For a great fried tomato, in my opinion, you need only a few ingredients—cornmeal, egg, sea salt, spices, lemon, and a perfectly ripe summer tomato.

SERVES 8 In a small bowl, whisk together the egg, buttermilk, and hot sauce.

Add ¼ cup [35 g] of the flour to a plate. On a second plate, combine the cornmeal, remaining ¼ cup [35 g] of flour, and kosher salt and mix together.

Dredge each tomato slice in the plain flour, shaking off any excess, then dip in the egg mixture and dredge in the cornmeal mixture. Make sure the tomatoes are evenly coated.

In a Dutch oven or heavy-bottomed pot, heat the oil to 365°F [185°C]. Monitor the temperature with a candy thermometer or digital thermometer. Set up a rack or tray with layered paper towels.

Working in batches, carefully add the tomatoes to the oil, cooking on each side for about 1½ minutes, or until golden brown and crispy. Transfer to the paper towels to drain in single layers. Season with sea salt and splash with fresh lemon juice. Serve hot.

RICE AND GRAVY

FOR THE GRAVY

2 chicken carcasses

3 whole garlic heads

2 onions, coarsely chopped

2 carrots, coarsely chopped

2 celery stalks, coarsely chopped

8 cups [2 L] chicken broth

1 Tbsp finely chopped fresh thyme

2 bay leaves

Hot sauce

Kosher salt and freshly cracked black pepper

⅓ cup [45 g] all-purpose flour

⅓ cup [80 ml] vegetable oil

FOR THE RICE

2 cups [400 g] white rice

2 Tbsp butter

1 tsp kosher salt

Chopped fresh parsley, for serving (optional)

If you want to change up the serving sizes, keep this ratio in mind: 2 cups [480 ml] of water for every 1 cup [200 g] of uncooked rice equals 3 cups [360 g] of cooked rice.

SERVES 6   *To make the gravy:* Preheat the oven to 350°F [180°C]. Place the chicken carcasses, garlic, onion, carrots, and celery in a roasting pan and roast for 1 hour, or until the bones take on a rich brown color. Transfer the contents of the roasting pan (including the rendered fat) to a stockpot. Add the chicken broth, thyme, and bay leaves. Bring to a simmer and cook, uncovered, for 2 hours.

Strain and discard the solids and return the strained liquid to the pot. Season the liquid with the hot sauce, salt, and pepper. In a bowl, stir together the flour and vegetable oil until thoroughly combined. Slowly stream this slurry into the hot liquid, stirring, until it reaches a gravy consistency and coats the back of a spoon, 5 to 8 minutes.

Transfer any unused gravy to airtight containers. Let cool completely to room temperature, then refrigerate. It will keep, refrigerated, for up to 2 weeks, or frozen for up to 2 months.

To make the rice: Bring 4 cups [960 ml] of water to a boil in a medium saucepan. Add the rice, butter, and salt. Stir to combine. Lower the heat to low, cover the rice, and let it simmer for 20 minutes. Remove from the heat and fluff with a fork.

To serve, portion rice onto plates and spoon hot gravy over the top. Sprinkle with chopped parsley, if desired.

OKRA AND TOMATO STEW

½ cup [115 g] diced slab bacon

1 onion, finely diced

½ cup [60 g] finely diced celery

4 cups [900 g] sliced okra

One 15 oz [430 g] can diced tomatoes

One 15 oz [430 g] can stewed tomatoes

¾ cup [180 ml] chicken stock

2 tsp Cajun seasoning

2 Tbsp hot sauce

½ tsp garlic powder

Salt and freshly cracked black pepper

3 Tbsp chopped fresh parsley

I used this stew to bulk out multiple dishes at Butterfunk Kitchen, from the oxtails to the shrimp and grits (although it's delicious on its own, over rice). I think Nana would be proud that I've figured out how to stretch food, in order to stretch a dollar.

SERVES 6   Add the bacon to a medium Dutch oven over medium heat. Cook until crispy, about 5 minutes.

Add the onion and celery and cook until tender, about 5 minutes.

Add the okra, tomatoes, stock, Cajun seasoning, hot sauce, and garlic powder. Simmer for 30 minutes, uncovered, stirring occasionally.

Season with salt and pepper, sprinkle with the parsley, and serve.

CABBAGE SOUP WITH EGG NOODLES AND SMOKED HAM HOCK

½ cup [115 g] fatback or slab bacon

1 cup [140 g] finely diced onion

1 cup [140 g] finely diced carrot

1 cup [120 g] finely diced celery

1 Tbsp minced garlic

8 cups [2 L] chicken stock

3 smoked ham hocks

1 tsp dried thyme

1 dried bay leaf

Kosher salt and freshly cracked black pepper

1 cup [225 g] peeled and diced starchy potato (like russet)

1 green cabbage, cut into 8 wedges

1 lb [455 g] egg noodles

3 Tbsp butter

As long as she had a little smoked meat lying around, Nana could generally pull together this dish. You could eat as much soup as you wanted, but the egg noodles were what everyone was after—those had to be rationed out.

SERVES 8   Add the fatback or slab bacon to a Dutch oven or stockpot over medium heat. Cook until the fat is rendered, about 15 minutes. Add the onion, carrot, celery, and garlic. Cook for 5 minutes, or until translucent. Add the chicken stock, ham hocks, thyme, bay leaf, salt, pepper, and potato, which will thicken the soup as it cooks. Cover and cook for 30 minutes. Add the cabbage wedges and lower to a simmer. Cook for 25 minutes more.

Meanwhile, bring a pot of water to a boil and add the egg noodles. Cook until just tender, about 8 minutes. Drain and toss with the butter. Place the egg noodles in individual bowls and ladle the cabbage soup over the top.

PAN-SEARED CHICKEN LIVERS

1 cup [140 g] all-purpose flour

1½ tsp kosher salt

1 tsp freshly cracked black pepper

½ tsp smoked paprika

2 lb [910 g] chicken livers, rinsed and drained

¼ cup [60 ml] bacon fat or oil

We'd pair our livers with Low Country Potato Salad (page 122) and hot sauce, but you can eat them in a salad or over rice or cheese grits (see page 73), teamed with your choice of chow-chow. *Note:* You can use the drippings to make a Brown Milk Gravy (see page 83).

SERVES 6   Combine the flour, salt, pepper, and paprika in a mixing bowl. Dredge the livers until they are completely coated with the flour mixture.

Heat the bacon fat over medium-high heat in a large skillet. Layer a plate with paper towels. Gently add the livers in batches, searing on one side for 3 to 4 minutes, then cooking on the other side for 2 minutes more. Remove from the pan and let drain on paper towels. Serve hot or at room temperature.

CHICKEN BACKS AND TURNIP STEW

2 chicken backs, cut into 2 in [5 cm] pieces

1 onion, finely diced

3 celery stalks, finely diced

2 large carrots, unpeeled and finely diced

2 garlic cloves, minced

2 potatoes, peeled and finely diced

3 turnips, peeled and finely diced

Kosher salt and freshly cracked black pepper

The chicken back—the piece that's left after the breasts, thighs, legs, and wings have been removed—has only a bit of skin and very little meat. It's mostly bone, and when I was growing up, we would suck on those bones, gently cracking them open with our teeth, to release any marrow and get as many nutrients as we could.

SERVES 6 Add all the ingredients to a large stockpot along with 12 cups [2.8 L] of cold water, and bring to a boil. Once boiling, lower the heat to medium and simmer, covered, for 45 minutes.

Remove from the heat and serve in bowls, bones and all.

CHICKEN AND DUMPLINGS

One 3 lb [1.4 kg] chicken, giblets removed

1 cup [140 g] coarsely chopped carrots

½ cup [60 g] coarsely chopped celery

½ cup [70 g] coarsely chopped onion

¼ cup [50 g] sugar

1 Tbsp chopped fresh rosemary

Kosher salt and freshly cracked black pepper

1 recipe Brown Sugar Buttermilk Biscuit dough (not baked) (page 218)

This is one of my favorite Amish dishes, right up there with chicken corn soup. Unlike Southern-style dumplings, Pennsylvania Dutch dumplings are flat and super chewy, in a good way, and are perfect for soaking up all that rich, chicken-y goodness. As for my dumplings, I actually use my famous biscuit recipe and poach the dough in the broth to make little puffy clouds.

SERVES 8   Put the chicken and vegetables into a stockpot with enough water to cover. Bring to a boil, covered, over high heat, then lower to a simmer and cook for 1 hour.

Strain the stock and return the liquid to the stockpot. Discard the veggies and transfer the chicken to a dish to cool.

When the chicken is cool, tear the meat and skin into bite-size pieces. Return to the pot and bring to a simmer over medium-high heat. Add the sugar and rosemary and season with salt and pepper.

While the broth is simmering, pinch off ½ oz [15 g] balls of biscuit dough and add them to the stock. Cook for 30 minutes and serve.

Note: Don't throw out that carcass! Freeze and save for use in recipes such as Chicken Backs and Turnip Stew (page 156) or Rice and Gravy (page 149).

TURKEY NECK GUMBO OVER RICE

½ cup [120 ml] vegetable or canola oil

3 cups [420 g] finely diced onion

3 cups [360 g] finely diced green bell peppers

3 cups [360 g] finely diced red bell peppers

3 cups [360 g] finely diced celery

3 Tbsp minced garlic

18 turkey necks

1 cup [140 g] all-purpose flour

3 Tbsp filé powder (available in specialty stores or online)

12 cups [2.8 L] chicken stock

1 Tbsp dried thyme

Kosher salt and freshly cracked black pepper

Hot sauce

Cooked white rice, for serving

Around Thanksgiving, Nana would stock up on turkey necks. And whatever she didn't use for gravy, she'd freeze for gumbo. We always knew to expect this dish shortly after the holiday, since the celebration generally left us too broke to splurge on fancy food.

SERVES 8   In a large Dutch oven, heat the oil over medium heat. Add the onion, bell peppers, celery, and garlic and cook for 3 minutes, or until translucent. Add the turkey necks and caramelize for about 8 minutes. Remove the necks from the pot and set aside. Add the flour and filé powder to the pot to make a roux and stir continuously for 25 minutes, until it is dark brown.

Return the turkey necks to the pot along with the chicken stock and thyme. Stir and bring to a boil over high heat. Lower the heat to a simmer, cover, and cook for 1 hour.

Skim the excess fat off the top of the gumbo. Season with salt, pepper, and hot sauce and serve over the rice.

THE BEAUTY OF BONES

When you literally have only a couple of dollars to put toward food, purchasing inexpensive bones for a hearty stock is a great option. Whether they're beef, pork, chicken, or fish, you'll want to blanch your bones before roasting or simmering them. This removes the impurities that float and foam on the top, which are colorfully referred to as "scum." Simply cover the bones with cold water, boil for 15 minutes, then drain completely, discarding all the bad water and giving your bones a final rinse.

The gelatin in the bones helps make your final broth thick and viscous. Have your butcher cut the bones into small pieces to get as much marrow flavor as possible and allow the natural collagen to be easily released.

NECKBONE DUMPLINGS

FOR THE NECKBONE STEW

3 Tbsp vegetable or canola oil

2 lb [910 g] pork neckbones, cut into 2 in [5 cm] pieces (your butcher can do this)

1 onion, diced small

3 carrots, unpeeled and finely diced

3 celery stalks, finely diced

3 garlic cloves, minced

½ cup [70 g] all-purpose flour

2 large tomatoes, chopped

Kosher salt and freshly cracked black pepper

FOR THE DUMPLINGS

3 cups [420 g] all-purpose flour

2 tsp baking powder

1 tsp kosher salt

½ cup [120 ml] vegetable or canola oil

2 eggs

1 Tbsp finely chopped fresh parsley

3 Tbsp butter

One of the few good memories I have of my father (who abandoned us for good when I was only seven) was when he took me "crabbin'" down in Beaufort, South Carolina, where he grew up. He'd take a neckbone, tie a string around it, and throw it in the water, where it would be immediately surrounded by a cluster of blue crabs. Those crabs were a treat—and so was actually spending time with my dad.

But for the most part, the neckbone was more relevant to my days. As meager as it was, it taught me to be grateful just to have something. To know how to make a meal out of practically nothing. To be able to say, at least we have meat today. *Note:* Ask your butcher to cut up the neckbones for you.

SERVES 8 *To make the stew:* In a Dutch oven, heat the oil over high heat. Add the neckbones and stir occasionally until caramelized, about 8 minutes. Add the onions, carrots, celery, and garlic. Keep stirring until the vegetables begin to get color, about 5 minutes. Stir in the flour and stir until the flour gets slightly golden, about 4 minutes. Add the tomatoes and 10 cups [2.4 L] of water, and season with salt and pepper. Cover with a lid and cook over medium heat for 1½ hours.

cont'd

To make the dumplings: Sift the flour, baking powder, and salt into a mixing bowl. In a separate bowl, combine the oil, eggs, parsley, and ¾ cup [180 ml] of cold water and pour into the dry ingredients. Using your hands, work the mixture together and knead it until a dough ball forms. Separate the dough ball into two equal portions.

Dust a tabletop and a baking sheet with flour. Working one ball at a time, roll out the dough on the tabletop into a flat rectangle, about ½ in [12 mm] thick. Cut strips, then cut each strip into ½ in [12 mm] cubes. Set the cubes on the baking sheet and repeat the process with the second dough ball. Once you have all the dough cubes, bring a pot of salted water to a boil. Lower the heat to a medium-high simmer and, working in batches, drop the dumplings in the boiling water and blanch them for 3 to 5 minutes, until they float. Lift out with a slotted spoon and put directly on a clean baking sheet to cool down.

In a cast-iron skillet over medium heat, melt the butter until golden brown, about 3 minutes. Working in batches, add the dumplings to the skillet and cook until lightly browned, about 4 minutes. Transfer the dumplings to a large serving bowl. Spoon the neck-bone stew over the dumplings and serve immediately.

PIG'S FEET AND POTATOES

2 Tbsp vegetable or canola oil

¼ cup [55 g] minced garlic

½ cup [60 g] diced red bell peppers

½ cup [70 g] diced onion

1 carrot, unpeeled and diced

3 Tbsp ground cumin

1 Tbsp ground coriander

1½ cups [360 ml] tomato sauce

4 cups [960 ml] chicken stock

3 lb [1.4 kg] pig's feet, quartered (your butcher can do this for you)

3 Yukon gold potatoes, peeled and diced

¼ cup [10 g] chopped fresh cilantro

Cooked rice, for serving

Hot sauce, for serving

This was one of the few dishes my Grandpop ever made, inspired by his Sicilian mother. Those flavors always came through when he cooked—as in a spaghetti-and-meat-sauce dish our family took to calling "slumgullion." It was also one of the few dishes my mother prepared. She was in the habit of eating the pig's feet right out of the pot, accompanied by a big ole thing of Crystal hot sauce.

SERVES 6   In a medium pot, heat the oil over medium-high heat. Add the garlic, peppers, and onion. Stir until softened, about 3 minutes. Add the carrot, cumin, and coriander and cook until the spices are fragrant, about 2 minutes. Add the tomato sauce, chicken stock, and pig's feet. Bring to a boil, then lower to a simmer, cover, and cook for 1½ hours.

Add the potatoes and cook for 30 to 45 minutes more, uncovered, or until the meat pulls easily from the bones. Stir in the cilantro. Serve over rice with hot sauce.

RICE AND RESILIENCE

As a parent of four beautiful people, I always want to be the best I can be. I want to inspire and to help open life's doors for them. I want to pass down traditions and tell family stories, make them proud to be in their own skin and celebrate who they are. I want them to be participants in this world, and to work hand-in-hand with others to make it a better place.

I'm sure my mother felt this too as she was raising me. But when you're a child, you don't realize the struggle that often comes at the expense of support. Sometimes, it takes walking their walk to relate to the hardships of others. Living through some tough times myself as an adult gave me a deeper understanding of what my mother was going through.

I now understand why she was so pissed off most of the time. Having an abusive relationship with my father led her to move back in with her mother, child in tow, just to make ends meet. She had to give up many of her dreams, simply to make mine come true. She took any job that paid a somewhat decent wage to keep clothes on my back and food on the table. And when she had cancer, she still had to work, because we were broke.

But I couldn't see then, or understand, what she was going through. I was confused when she would curse me out while making dinner, because of something I did or didn't do. I was surprised when I'd receive beatings because I was stubborn or wouldn't listen to her. It was all she could do to not simply give up and walk away from all of us. Now that I'm a parent, I'm sure she felt horrible treating me like that, talking to me in ways that killed my spirit, and giving me a complex I carry to this day. Just as I'm sure it was frustrating when she couldn't provide a balanced dinner for her child.

I know now that she did the best that she could with what she had. That's what my recipe for Rice and Gravy (page 149) is about. Sometimes the cupboards would be bare except for a few essentials, but Mom would still find a way to make this. Occasionally with tears running down her face. Maybe out of anger. Maybe out of frustration. And she'd sit silently in front of the TV, eating her bowl of rice and gravy.

CRISPY FRIED TRIPE WITH HOT VINEGAR PEPPERS

2 lb [910 g] honeycomb tripe

1 cup [140 g] all-purpose flour

2 Tbsp smoked paprika

1½ tsp kosher salt

1 tsp baking powder

4 cups [946 ml] canola oil

Hot pickled peppers, for serving

Nana would serve tripe pieces in a vinegary, spicy broth, with a few veggies. I hated it. It wasn't until I got older that I began to see tripe pop up at a lot of restaurants I respected, so I decided to revisit it. I knew I needed to do something about the texture, though, so I came up with this preparation. Tripe can be found at many Caribbean markets.

SERVES 4 Prepare a salted ice bath. In a medium pot, bring 6 cups [1.4 L] of salted water to a boil. Add the tripe and cook for 4 minutes. Remove from the hot water and shock in the salted ice water. Once cooled, slice the cooked tripe into 1 in [2.5 cm] long strips, and set aside.

On a plate, mix together the flour, paprika, salt, and baking powder. In a Dutch oven or heavy-bottomed pot, heat the oil to 350°F [180°C]. Layer paper towels on a plate. Working in batches, dredge the tripe slices in the flour mixture and gently place them in the hot oil. Deep-fry until golden brown, about 2 minutes.

Transfer the tripe to the paper towels to drain off excess oil and serve with sliced pickled hot peppers and their vinegar.

DANDELION WINE

3 lb [1.4 kg] sugar

4 lb [1.8 kg] dandelion blossoms, washed

2 tsp cake yeast

1 cup [240 ml] fresh orange juice

1 cup [240 ml] fresh lemon juice

8 cups [2 L] cheap brandy or whiskey

On summer nights when my grandparents entertained friends, they'd pull out the card table and the "nice" folding chairs with the cushions. Old-school music would come from a speaker propped up right by the window, so the sound would travel outside. And Nana would bring out a treat that she'd been working on for weeks—dandelion wine.

When you can't really afford to buy hooch, you make do with what's around. And what could be cheaper than fermenting those weeds that spring up between the street cracks? Not that that made this wine any less special. Seeing my grandparents together and happy made me happy. And it cemented this wine as one of my feel-good memories, with me on the perimeter of their fun, catching fireflies.

MAKES 1 GALLON [3.8 L] In a large pot, bring 3 qt [2.8 L] of water to a boil. Add the sugar and stir until dissolved. Place the dandelion blossoms in a large, lidded container, and pour the water mixture over the top. Let steep overnight at room temperature.

The next day, add the yeast. Stir to dissolve, cover, and store at room temperature for 1 week. After a week, strain and discard the blossoms, reserving the liquid. Combine the liquid with the orange juice, lemon juice, and brandy. Bottle in a 1 gal [3.8 L] jug and refrigerate for up to 2 months.

CHAPTER 5

Celebration Foods

In the Black communities that I grew up in, Sundays normally began with church service. If you grew up in a Black church the way I did, then you probably remember the almost two-hour sermons and the exhilarating music of the choir. Nana would give me peppermint candies out of her pocketbook just so I would sit still. She'd also seat us in the front row, so if I did act out or fall asleep, the whole congregation would see me.

After church service, we'd head down to the church basement, where all of the old ladies would be in their plastic disposable aprons serving up homemade goodies like fried chicken, macaroni salad, ambrosia Jell-O salad, and strawberry Kool-Aid. Just enough to tide you over until you got home for the big family dinner.

Storytelling was an important part of the day too. We'd talk about our ancestors and various eras of Black America. It was also a time to make peace with one another, to quash all gossip and start fresh. A time to reconnect as a family and as a community. As time went on, this Sunday tradition of reconnection seeped into celebrations such as weddings, birthdays, graduations, and all major holidays.

On Sundays and these special occasions, it was customary to bust out high-end ingredients we normally couldn't enjoy every day of the week. To poor Black folks back in the day, items like butter, sugar, chicken, or any kind of animal protein were luxuries.

Many people still think of "celebration" dishes as food Black folks ate on the regular. But as far as things like red velvet cake go—well, we were too broke and too damn busy trying to get reasonably nourishing meals on the table to be dyeing our food red just for fun.

Even if celebration foods were far from being everyday indulgences, their history extends all the way back to slavery. Sundays were when slaves could, if their request was granted, visit kinfolk on other plantations. So they would prepare meals that expressed love and appreciation for family and friends. That shared time also allowed them to pass down their knowledge on the intricate preparations of celebratory dishes to the next generation. And that's how fried chicken, BBQ beef and pork, biscuits, pies, and cakes all worked their way into the culture.

CRISPY DEVILED EGGS WITH CRACKLIN' COLLARD GREENS

8 eggs from a cardboard, not Styrofoam, carton (keep the carton)

1 tsp baking soda

1 tsp kosher salt, plus more as needed

6 Tbsp [90 g] mayonnaise

1 tsp mustard

1 tsp sugar

2 Tbsp flour

1 cup [140 g] seasoned Italian bread crumbs

4 cups [960 ml] vegetable or canola oil

1 collard green leaf, stems stripped out, leaves cut into 1 in [2.5 cm] pieces, well dried

These deviled eggs damn near became the face of my restaurant. They're so photogenic, and influencers from all around went gaga over them. You'll definitely be the talk of all your friends if you serve these eggs at your next cocktail party or soiree.

SERVES 4 Place 6 of the eggs in a pot, with enough cold water to cover completely. Add the baking soda and salt. Cover and bring to a boil over high heat, then lower to medium-high and cook for 8 minutes. Remove the eggs from the pot and shock them in ice water. Peel the eggs immediately and cut them in half horizontally. Carefully remove the yolks and put them in a bowl. Add the mayonnaise, mustard, and sugar and season with salt. Whisk together until totally smooth and free of lumps. Transfer the filling to a pastry bag and refrigerate for 1 hour. Rinse the empty whites in cold water.

In a bowl, whisk together the remaining 2 eggs and the flour. Put the bread crumbs in a separate bowl. Dip the hard-boiled egg white halves in the egg-flour mixture and then the bread crumbs, making sure they're completely and evenly coated, inside and out.

In a small saucepan, heat the oil to 350°F [180°C]. Gently place the breaded egg whites in the oil and deep-fry until golden brown all around, about 3 minutes total. Arrange the breaded egg whites, cup-side up, in the egg carton.

Layer paper towels on a rack. Making sure the oil is still at 350°F [180°C], add the collard green pieces. The oil will likely splatter, so you may want to use a splatter guard or lid. As soon as the pieces get crispy (it literally takes about 5 seconds), remove with a slotted metal spoon. Drain on the paper towels and season with salt.

To serve, using the piping bag, evenly divide the filling among the fried cups. Garnish each with a fried collard chip.

MACARONI AND CHEESE

½ cup [113 g] butter

½ cup [70 g] all-purpose flour

5 cups [1.2 L] milk

3 Tbsp garlic powder

4 cups [120 g] coarsely grated Parmesan cheese

1 lb [455 g] macaroni shells, cooked according to package directions

3 cups [240 g] shredded Monterey Jack cheese

3 cups [240 g] shredded Cheddar cheese

This recipe won *Time Out New York* magazine's "Best Mac and Cheese" contest back in 2017. It has an awesome, crusty, golden-brown top and the ooey-gooiest center known to humankind. I like using medium pasta shells, which allow the cheese and béchamel to thoroughly coat the outsides as well as really work their way into the nooks and crannies.

SERVES 8 Preheat the oven to 350°F [180°C].

In a large saucepan over medium heat, melt the butter. Add the flour, whisking constantly, until thoroughly combined and lightly browned, about 5 minutes. Add the milk and garlic powder, bring to a boil, and lower to a simmer. Cook until a creamy béchamel forms, 6 to 8 minutes. Turn off the heat and whisk in the Parmesan cheese, stirring until thoroughly combined.

Fold the cooked macaroni shells into the béchamel, then pour into an ungreased baking dish.

In a bowl, combine the Monterey Jack and Cheddar cheese. Sprinkle evenly over the casserole. Bake for 40 minutes, or until the cheese is melted and the top is golden brown.

A PASTA FAUX PAS

Pouring oil into pasta cooking water is a pet peeve of mine, because nothing will stick to oily pasta, especially not a gooey, slithery cheese sauce. Apply oil, if needed, after cooking only, as in the dressing for a cold pasta salad.

JACKFRUIT HAND PIES

2 cups [455 g] canned jackfruit, rinsed and drained

½ cup [130 g] ketchup

¼ cup [80 g] molasses

3 Tbsp mustard

3 Tbsp liquid smoke

2 Tbsp packed brown sugar

2 tsp smoked paprika

1 tsp freshly cracked black pepper

½ tsp kosher salt

1 Tbsp vegetable oil

1 onion, finely diced

3 sheets frozen puff pastry, defrosted

1 cup [80 g] shredded Cheddar cheese

Jackfruit is grown in Southeast Asia and tastes like a blend of pineapple, banana, and mango. It can be used in either sweet or savory preparations, boiled to make custard, or cooked into curry. And it's emerged as a bit of a hero among vegans and vegetarians, as it has a unique texture that allows it to approximate meat. That was my thinking here—using jackfruit to make a meatless, West Indian–inspired hand pie.

SERVES 4   Preheat the oven to 350°F [180°C].

Using your hands, shred the jackfruit into strands. In a bowl, mix with the ketchup, molasses, mustard, liquid smoke, brown sugar, paprika, pepper, and salt.

Heat the oil in a sauté pan over medium heat. Add the onion and cook until translucent, about 3 minutes. Add the jackfruit and cook for 15 minutes.

With a round cookie cutter (3 to 4 in [7.5 to 10 cm]), cut circles from the puff pastry. Place 2 Tbsp of jackfruit mix in the middle of each circle. Evenly divide the Cheddar among the circles and fold them over empanada style. Crimp the edges with a fork. Bake for 15 to 20 minutes, or until puffed and golden brown. Cool on a wire rack.

Serve warm or at room temperature. Store leftover pies at room temperature in an airtight container for up to 2 days. Reheat in a 325°F [165°C] oven for 8 to 10 minutes.

STUFFED CHARD WITH SWEET POTATOES AND BLACK RICE

FOR THE SWEET POTATOES

3 Tbsp olive oil

3 sweet potatoes, peeled and finely diced

½ cup [70 g] finely diced onion

2 tsp kosher salt

2 tsp ground cumin

2 tsp chili powder

1 Tbsp tomato paste

1 cup [240 ml] vegetable broth

FOR THE BLACK RICE

1 cup [200 g] black rice

2½ cups [600 ml] vegetable broth

2 tsp kosher salt

1 bunch rainbow Swiss chard (or any kind of hearty leafy green, such as collards or kale), stems cut off and sliced thinly, leaves kept whole

FOR THE COCONUT CURRY SAUCE

One 15 oz [425 g] can coconut milk

¼ cup [60 ml] fresh lime juice

3 Tbsp curry paste

2 Tbsp brown sugar

2 garlic cloves

2 Tbsp chopped fresh cilantro

Kosher salt

When you have powerhouse items like fried chicken and ribs hogging the spotlight, it takes a lot of doing to wow without meat. But Southern cuisine is built on a strong agricultural foundation. So I think it's high time that vegetables got their due. Besides, I think any time you add an exciting vegetarian or vegan dish to a classic soul food menu, you've got ample reason to celebrate. *Note:* Be sure to use black rice, not wild rice—that's totally different.

SERVES 4 *To make the sweet potatoes:* In a sauté pan, heat the oil over medium heat. Add the sweet potatoes, onion, salt, cumin, and chili powder. Stir continuously for 8 to 10 minutes, or until the potatoes are tender. Add the tomato paste and broth. Cook, stirring, for 5 minutes more. Set aside.

To make the rice: In a medium saucepan over medium-high heat, add the rice and vegetable broth and bring to a boil. Add the salt, lower the heat to a simmer, and cover. Cook for 45 minutes to 1 hour, or until tender.

cont'd

Note: If you rinse and soak black rice before using, you can decrease the cooking time to 20 to 30 minutes.

Let the cooked rice stay covered for 5 minutes off the heat. Uncover and fluff with a fork. Transfer the hot rice to a mixing bowl and fold in the sweet potato mixture. Add the chard stems to the filling and stir to combine. Set the filling aside.

Fill a medium stockpot halfway with salted water and bring to a boil. Lower the heat to a simmer. Prepare a large bowl of salted ice water.

Place two of the chard leaves at a time in the simmering water. Let them blanch for no longer than 15 seconds, then use a slotted spoon to transfer them right into the ice bath. Repeat this process with the remaining leaves.

Transfer the leaves to a colander to drain. Preheat the oven to 350°F [180°C].

Gently squeeze the excess water from each leaf, being careful not to rip the leaf. Lay each leaf flat, totally open. Place about ¼ cup [55 g] of filling ½ in [12 mm] from the stem end of each leaf. Roll up like cigars and place in a baking dish.

To make the curry sauce: In a food processor, process all the ingredients together until smooth.

Pour the sauce over the chard rolls and bake for 30 minutes, or until hot. Serve hot or at room temperature, spooning the sauce on top of the rolls.

SOFTSHELL CRABS WITH SOUR CORN AND LADY CREAM PEA SALAD

FOR THE SOUR CORN

2 cups [480 ml] spring or filtered water

1½ Tbsp kosher salt

½ tsp red pepper flakes

4 ears fresh corn, kernels cut off of the cob (about 3 cups [480 g])

FOR THE LADY CREAM PEAS

¼ cup [55 g] diced slab bacon

1 small onion, diced

2 garlic cloves, minced

1¼ cups [200 g] dried lady cream peas or black-eyed peas or white beans, soaked for 24 hours

4 cups [960 ml] chicken stock

Kosher salt and freshly cracked black pepper

FOR THE CRABS

1½ cups [210 g] all-purpose flour

3 Tbsp Old Bay seasoning

8 softshell crabs, cleaned (see sidebar, page 184)

4 Tbsp butter

Fresh lemon juice, for serving (optional)

Softshell crab season generally lasts from mid-April until the end of August. Some purveyors sell through autumn, but the crabs are smaller, and the shells aren't so soft.

Lady cream peas are small white cowpeas. Southerners often serve them with corn, in a sort-of succotash. This is where inspiration caught me: summertime, seafood, fresh corn, Amish fermentation practices. This corn could well be listed among the Seven Sweets and Sours, and enjoyed as such. Left to sit for a week, it takes on a briny, funky, fermented flavor but is still crisp and sweet. *Note:* It will take a week to ferment the sour corn, so plan ahead.

SERVES 4   *To make the corn:* In a small saucepan over medium heat, combine the water and salt. Heat until the salt is just dissolved. Remove from the heat and let cool to about 100°F [35°C]. Add the red pepper flakes. This is your brine.

cont'd

HOW TO CLEAN SOFTSHELL CRABS

While softshell crabs do come frozen and already cleaned, I don't recommend purchasing them like this. When they defrost, they turn into a brown glob with the texture of a dirty dish towel. You want the fresh ones, still alive and kicking when you buy them.

First, cut off the "face." Don't cut too deeply, because you want to leave some crab to eat. Next, locate the gills under each wing and simply tear them out. Finally, tear off the belly flap. Done.

Transfer the corn kernels to sterilized mason jars. Pour in enough brine to cover the kernels by an inch or two. Place small ziplock bags filled with either water or the remaining brine on top of the kernels to keep them submerged. Cover the jars with cheesecloth or paper towels secured with string or rubber bands. Move to a cool, dark place for a week. Check daily and skim off any foam that forms. After a week, drain away the brine and transfer the sour corn to a mixing bowl.

To make the peas: In a pot over medium-high heat, cook the bacon until crisp, 6 to 8 minutes. Add the onion and garlic and cook until translucent, about 5 minutes. Drain the soaked peas and add them along with the stock to the pot with the bacon. Bring to a boil, then lower to a simmer. Cover the pot with a lid and cook for 1 hour, or until the peas are tender. Drain the peas. Add the pea mixture to the bowl of sour corn. Fold together, season with salt and pepper, and set aside.

Note: This salad will last for up to 4 days, refrigerated in an airtight container. When ready to finish the dish, remove from the refrigerator and let come to room temperature before proceeding.

To make the crabs: In a bowl, combine the flour and Old Bay seasoning. Dredge the crabs in the flour, coating evenly on all sides. Layer a plate with paper towels. In a sauté pan over high heat, melt the butter. When hot, add the crabs, shell-side down, working in batches if needed. When the shell side is bright orange and crispy, after 3 to 4 minutes, flip to the other side and cook for about 30 seconds. Transfer to the paper towels to drain.

To serve, place about 4 oz [115 g] of room-temperature pea salad on each plate and top with 2 softshell crabs. Finish with a squeeze of lemon, if desired.

BUTTER CRACKER–CRUSTED PERCH
WITH SWEET-AND-SOUR GREEN AND WAX BEANS

6 perch fillets or other flaky white fish

2 eggs, beaten

2 cups [455 g] finely crushed butter crackers

2 Tbsp butter

¼ cup [60 ml] blended oil (or half vegetable oil, half olive oil)

1 recipe Sweet-and-Sour Green and Wax Beans (page 61)

Like catfish and whiting, perch is an inexpensive yet delicious fish to fry and easy to find in markets and restaurants in predominantly African American communities.

SERVES 6   Dredge the perch in the egg. Dip into the crushed crackers until totally covered with crumbs adhering completely.

Heat the butter and oil in a sauté pan over medium-high heat. Line a plate with paper towels. Add the perch fillets and cook for 3 to 4 minutes on each side, or until golden brown. Transfer to the paper towels to drain.

To serve, divide the beans among plates and top each with a perch fillet.

CRISPY CORNMEAL CATFISH WITH HOT-PEPPER LEMON BUTTER

FOR THE CATFISH

1 cup [240 ml] buttermilk

¼ cup [60 ml] hot sauce

6 catfish fillets

½ cup [70 g] all-purpose flour

1½ cups [210 g] cornmeal

2 Tbsp kosher salt

2 tsp freshly cracked black pepper

2 tsp garlic powder

2 tsp smoked paprika

1 tsp dried thyme

1 tsp celery seed

6 cups [1.4 L] peanut or canola oil

FOR THE HOT-PEPPER LEMON BUTTER

One 12 oz [355 ml] bottle hot-pepper sauce

1 cup [240 ml] shrimp or fish stock

¾ cup [180 ml] fresh lemon juice

¼ cup [60 ml] cider vinegar

½ cup [100 g] sugar

3 Tbsp dashi powder or bonito flakes

1 cup [226 g] butter, cut into cubes

Nothing beats a good fish fry. There's something about sitting outside on a metal chair with chipped paint, surrounded by good friends, eating some fried whiting (or in this case, catfish), along with hushpuppies, coleslaw, white bread, two types of hot sauce, and a big ole glass of pink lemonade.

This recipe calls for regular cornmeal, but feel free to get creative. I mean, we're talking about celebration foods here. If you can get your hands on some blue cornmeal, then go to town. And I especially love serving this fish over a generous helping of cheese grits (see page 73).

SERVES 6   *To make the catfish:* In a flat plastic container, combine the buttermilk and hot sauce. Submerge the catfish fillets in the marinade, cover, and refrigerate for 2 hours.

In a bowl, combine the flour, cornmeal, salt, pepper, garlic powder, smoked paprika, thyme, and celery seed.

Preheat the oven to 200°F [90°C]. In a Dutch oven or heavy-bottomed pot, heat the oil to 350°F [180°C]. Line a baking sheet with paper towels. Dredge the catfish in the flour mixture and place 2 fillets at a time in the hot oil. Deep-fry until golden brown, 2 to 3 minutes per side. Carefully transfer to the paper towels to drain, and keep warm in the oven.

To make the hot-pepper lemon butter: Add the hot-pepper sauce, stock, lemon juice, vinegar, sugar, dashi, and ½ cup [120 ml] of water to a medium saucepan. Bring to a boil over medium-high heat. Lower the heat to a simmer, and immediately whisk in the butter cubes until emulsified and slightly thick. Serve with the catfish.

CHICKEN AND WAFFLES "MY STYLE"

FOR THE CHICKEN LIVER MOUSSE

¼ cup [55 g] plus ½ cup [113 g] butter

1 onion, finely diced

3 Tbsp chopped fresh thyme

1 dried bay leaf

1 tsp black peppercorns

⅓ cup [80 ml] white wine

1 lb [455 g] chicken livers, rinsed and cleaned of sinew

½ tsp pink curing salt (not Himalayan pink salt)

½ cup [120 ml] heavy cream

Kosher salt

Olive oil, for topping

FOR THE CHICKEN HEARTS

1 cup [145 g] chicken hearts, rinsed

1 cup [240 ml] buttermilk

2 tsp liquid smoke

3 tsp kosher salt

½ cup [65 g] flour

2 tsp baking powder

4 cups [960 ml] canola oil

1 recipe Crispy Potato Waffles (page 69)

Yam Molasses (page 46) and hot sauce, for serving

Made with chicken liver mousse, potato waffles, yam molasses, and hot sauce, this dish doesn't contain leg, wing, thigh, or breast. I like using chicken hearts, marinated beforehand so they aren't so gamey, and fried up crisp, before being scattered over a savory waffle. Granted, this recipe has a lot of components. But the mousse gets made 24 hours ahead of time, and the rest comes together quickly after that.

SERVES 6   *To make the chicken liver mousse:* Melt the ¼ cup [55 g] of the butter in a sauté pan over medium heat. Add the onions and cook until translucent, about 5 minutes. Add the thyme, bay leaf, and peppercorns and cook for 1 minute. Add the wine and cook until the liquid is reduced by half, about 2 minutes. Set aside to cool for about 10 minutes.

Once the mixture is cool to the touch, remove the bay leaf. Transfer the mixture to a blender and purée until completely smooth. Transfer the purée to a bowl and set aside.

In another bowl, dredge the livers in the curing salt until the livers are evenly coated. Let sit for 10 minutes. Meanwhile, melt the remaining ½ cup [113 g] of butter and let cool to room temperature.

cont'd

Transfer the livers to the blender and purée until completely smooth. Add the heavy cream and melted butter. Purée to combine. Add to the bowl with the onions and fold together by hand. Transfer to a fine-mesh strainer set over a bowl and push the mousse through with a spoon, so the mousse is as silky as possible and any impurities are left in the strainer.

Divide the mousse into small mason jars, filling them about two-thirds of the way up, as the mousse will expand during cooking. Top with a thin coat of olive oil. This will help prevent the mousse from oxidizing.

Wrap the tops of the jars with plastic wrap and seal with the mason lids. Place the jars in the bottom of a large stockpot and fill with enough water to create steam when boiling. Bring to a boil, then lower the heat and simmer, covered, for 30 minutes.

Remove from the pot and carefully take off the jar lids. Let the mousse cool to room temperature. Once cool, place in the refrigerator for 24 hours. At that point the mousse is ready to serve or can be stored with the lids on, in the refrigerator, for up to 1 week.

To make the chicken hearts: In a large bowl, combine the chicken hearts, buttermilk, liquid smoke, and 2 tsp of the salt. Let sit for 1 hour. In another bowl, combine the flour, baking powder, and the remaining 1 tsp of salt.

Add the oil to a Dutch oven or heavy-bottomed pot and heat to 350°F [180°C]. Layer a baking sheet with paper towels. Dredge the chicken hearts in the flour mixture and add to the oil, working in batches if needed, and fry for 3 minutes or until crispy and evenly brown. Remove with a slotted spoon and drain on the paper towels.

To serve, put a hot waffle on each plate. Top with a heaping scoop of mousse (if you're up for making quenelles, they make a nice presentation) and a few of the chicken hearts. Drizzle with Yam Molasses and hot sauce.

THE PROBLEM WITH CHICKEN AND WAFFLES

I intentionally kept chicken and waffles off of my menu at Butter-funk Kitchen. Not because I didn't think it was delicious, and not because I thought it couldn't sell. But because I didn't like what I thought it represented.

John T. Edge calls chicken and waffles "a Southern dish, but a South-ern dish once or twice removed from the South." It attained wide-spread popularity at a time when white chefs began to gain traction for celebrating their Southern roots, although there were several African American chefs who were doing their thing as well but always remained in the shadows. Chicken and waffles, to me, repre-sented an appropriation of our dishes, our culture, and our story.

It wasn't until I began looking deeper that I found that Amish folk were actually eating stewed chicken on top of waffles or pancakes since way back in the early 1800s. It practically defined Pennsylva-nia Dutch food culture.

Knowing this loosened my stance on who has rights to what, and why. But I still couldn't bring myself to fully embrace the com-mercialized idea of chicken and waffles, which can be found in restaurants as rootless as IHOP and Chick-fil-A. My version is my love letter to the African American South, filtered through my fine dining background, with a nod to the methods and traditions of the Pennsylvania Dutch.

LEMONADE BUTTERMILK FRIED CHICKEN

FOR THE BRINE

1 cup [240 ml] fresh lemon juice

½ cup [120 ml] hot sauce

½ cup [25 g] garlic powder

½ cup [25 g] onion powder

½ cup [80 g] kosher salt

¼ cup [30 g] ground cumin

¼ cup [50 g] sugar

6 chicken drumsticks and 6 chicken thighs

1 cup [240 ml] buttermilk

1 cup [240 ml] Louisiana-style hot sauce

FOR THE BREADING

4 cups [560 g] all-purpose flour

1 cup [140 g] cornmeal

2 Tbsp baking powder

4 to 6 cups [960 ml to 1.4 L] vegetable or corn oil

"Brining" refers to the process of soaking meat in salted water. This not only adds flavor but also allows the meat to absorb some of that water after a long period (generally 12 to 24 hours), making it moister when cooked.

Now, when it comes to fried chicken, many Southern recipes favor a "sweet tea" brine, referencing the highly saccharine drink that's omnipresent in so many households. (Growing up, we dug sugary sweet drinks too, generally Kool-Aid or lemonade.) Rather than replicate a chicken recipe that everyone and their momma makes, I decided to come up with one that speaks to my family. My lemonade brine is as savory and tangy as it is sweet, and it has made this chicken a hit on a national scale. *Note:* You will need to start the brining process the day before.

MAKES 12 PIECES   *To make the brine:* In a large bowl, combine 8 cups [2 L] of cold water with the lemon juice, hot sauce, garlic powder, onion powder, salt, cumin, and sugar to make a brine. Stir until the salt and sugar are dissolved. Put the chicken pieces in a large plastic storage bag or other nonreactive container and cover with the brine. Refrigerate for 12 hours.

After 12 hours, remove the chicken from the brine and put into another clean plastic storage bag or container. Cover with the buttermilk and hot sauce and refrigerate for at least 2 to 6 hours.

cont'd

To make the breading: In a baking dish, combine the flour, cornmeal, and baking powder. Remove the chicken from the buttermilk and set on a rack to let the excess drip off. Dredge the pieces in the dry mix.

Fill a deep fryer or sauté pan with the oil and heat to 350°F [180°C]. Layer paper towels on a rack or baking sheet.

Carefully add the chicken pieces to the oil, cooking in batches if needed so as not to overcrowd the fryer or pan—you should be able to fit about 4 like-size pieces at a time, without causing the oil temperature to drop. Fry the chicken until cooked through and crispy, or until a meat thermometer inserted into the thickest point registers 165°F [75°C], 10 to 12 minutes. If the oil temperature drops below 325°F [165°C], raise the heat or fry fewer pieces at a time.

Remove the chicken from the oil and set on paper towels to dry. Serve immediately while hot.

THE STORY OF THE BIRDMAN

Slaves held many different positions on the plantation. Most were confined to fieldwork, and some worked as house slaves. A few men had skilled jobs, such as carpenters, coopers, blacksmiths, potters, and sugar boilers. Still others performed husbandry work, including cattlemen, hog boys, and birdmen.

The birdman was basically a chicken keeper, raising them from hatch to slaughter. He would provide the plantation with fresh eggs and live chickens to cook, and occasionally feathers as well, to manufacture blankets and pillows.

In 1692 the Virginia General Assembly, fearful that human chattel could eventually buy their freedom from profits made by selling animals, passed a law making it illegal for slaves to own horses, cattle, or pigs. As it was, slaves seldom had the opportunity to actually eat the animals they cared for, raised, and killed. They subsisted on whatever their owners gave them, which was usually scrap meat or offal. Stories on record show they were rarely permitted to take home leftovers from meals they had prepared at the Big House either. But the assembly didn't consider poultry worth mentioning in the law. And this loophole offered birdmen significant opportunity.

Most slaves originally hailed from West Africa, where there was a long history of raising chickens. And so, African Americans in the colonial South—both enslaved and free—eventually emerged as the general chicken merchants. At George Washington's home, Mount Vernon, slaves were actively forbidden to raise ducks or geese, making the chicken (as noted by one visitor) "the only pleasure allowed to Negroes." That pleasure was not just culinary, but also financial. In 1775, Thomas Jefferson paid two silver Spanish bits to slaves in exchange for three chickens. Such sales were very common. And since Black cooks were in a position to influence their masters' choice of dishes, they naturally favored the meat raised by their friends and relatives. One of the West African specialties that caught on among white people was chicken pieces fried in oil—a meal that now, around the world, is considered quintessentially American.

The course of history from there is clear. Slaves laid the foundation for America's abiding love affair with chicken.

SMOTHERED PORK CHOPS

1 cup [140 g] all-purpose flour

2 Tbsp blackening seasoning

1 Tbsp garlic powder

1 Tbsp onion powder

1 tsp smoked paprika

Four 10 oz [280 g] pork chops

3 Tbsp oil

2 onions, thinly sliced

3 Tbsp butter

1 cup [240 ml] chicken broth

2 cups [480 ml] cream

2 Tbsp fresh lemon juice

Kosher salt and freshly cracked black pepper

In my childhood household, pork and chicken were always washed in the sink before cooking. As they were sourced largely from corner stores and bodegas that sold subpar ingredients, this was something of a necessity. My mother loved this particular dish, so the few times I remember her making it, it would start with a brisk scrubbing of the pork in the sink. And once it was cooked, it was so well done (for our protection) that it really needed to be "smothered" to keep some form of moistness intact.

Needless to say, most of us have access to a much higher caliber of ingredients nowadays. I like bone-in pork, though you can use boneless if you'd rather. When you use bone-in pork, this classic soul food dish stays especially juicy. Although that shouldn't keep you from smothering on the sauce.

SERVES 4   In a bowl, combine ¼ cup [35 g] of the flour with the blackening seasoning, garlic powder, onion powder, and paprika. Evenly dredge all sides of the pork chops in the flour mixture.

Add the oil to a cast-iron skillet or sauté pan and heat over medium-high heat. Add the pork chops and sear until almost black, about 5 minutes on each side. Transfer to a plate.

Add the onions to the pan, turn down the heat to medium, and cook until caramelized, about 8 minutes. Add the butter and remaining ¾ cup [105 g] of flour to the pan and stir constantly until a brown roux forms, 8 to 10 minutes. Deglaze the pan with the chicken broth, cream, and lemon juice, stirring to scrape up the browned bits from the bottom of the pan.

Return the chops to the pan with the sauce and lower the heat to a medium-low simmer. Cover and cook for 20 minutes. Season with salt and pepper and serve immediately.

CHICKEN-FRIED STEAK WITH SASSAFRAS COUNTRY GRAVY

FOR THE STEAK

2 cups [480 ml] buttermilk

4 eggs

¼ cup [60 ml] hot sauce

4 cube steaks

1 cup [140 g] all-purpose flour

½ cup [70 g] cornstarch

1 Tbsp kosher salt

1 tsp baking powder

1 tsp garlic powder

½ tsp cayenne pepper

5 cups [1.2 L] vegetable or canola oil

FOR THE SASSAFRAS COUNTRY GRAVY

½ cup [70 g] finely diced onion

3 garlic cloves, minced

¼ cup [35 g] all-purpose flour

1 cup [240 ml] chicken broth

½ cup [120 ml] milk

¼ cup [60 ml] sassafras syrup (available online)

Kosher salt and freshly cracked black pepper

I once served this dish to my father-in-law. After a few bites, he signaled me over, asked me to bend down, and whispered in my ear, "This is steak, not chicken." I couldn't help but chuckle. My father-in-law is probably my biggest critic when it comes to food, not to mention my life in general. But hey, that's his job, right?

SERVES 4   *To make the steak:* In a shallow bowl, whisk together the buttermilk, eggs, and hot sauce. Submerge the meat in the buttermilk mixture and refrigerate for 1 hour.

In a shallow bowl, combine the flour, cornstarch, salt, baking powder, garlic powder, and cayenne. Dredge the steaks in the flour mixture, covering completely and knocking off any excess flour. Dip the steaks in the buttermilk marinade and then back into the flour mixture. Place on a baking sheet and let sit in the refrigerator for 20 minutes.

In a large Dutch oven or heavy-bottomed pot, heat the oil to 350°F [180°C]. Layer paper towels on a plate or rack. Add the steaks to the oil, one at a time, and fry until each side is golden brown, about 2 minutes per side. Place on the paper towels to drain.

To make the gravy: Transfer 2 Tbsp of the oil from the meat pan to a separate sauté pan. Set the heat to medium. Add the onions and garlic and cook until the onions are translucent, about 4 minutes. Add the flour and cook, stirring, for 2 to 3 minutes, or until the flour develops a very faint color. Stir in the broth, milk, and syrup and cook for 15 minutes, or until the gravy thickens. Season with salt and pepper.

Place a steak on each plate and spoon some of the sassafras gravy over the top. Serve hot.

BBQ RIBS WITH RHUBARB CHOW-CHOW

FOR THE RUB

1 Tbsp brown sugar

2 Tbsp smoked paprika

2 tsp kosher salt

1 tsp freshly cracked
black pepper

1 tsp onion powder

1 tsp garlic powder

1 tsp chili powder

1 tsp ground cumin

FOR THE RIBS

1 onion, sliced

4 garlic cloves, crushed

3 lb [1.4 kg] baby back ribs
(2 slabs)

Sea salt, for sprinkling

Rhubarb Chow-Chow
(page 50), for serving

Baby back ribs are my favorite dish to cook at home. They make it possible to actually cook BBQ in a tiny NYC apartment. And a couple of slabs feed a whole family. Just remember to peel the silver skin off the back of the ribs before cooking. And never boil them in advance, or you'll wash away all the flavor.

SERVES 6   Preheat the oven to 300°F [150°C].

To make the rub: In a small bowl, combine all the rub ingredients.

To make the ribs: Line a baking sheet with aluminum foil and evenly cover it with the onions and garlic. Remove the silver skin from the back of the rib rack. Rub the spice mixture all over the front and back of the ribs. Arrange the 2 slabs of ribs on top of the onions and garlic. Cover with more foil, wrapping each slab tightly. Bake the ribs for 2 hours.

After 2 hours, open one side of the foil to check for tenderness. The meat should be falling off of the bone. If not, rewrap and cook for 25 minutes more.

Discard the onions and garlic. Sprinkle the ribs with a little sea salt and grill or broil on high heat for 5 minutes. Serve with Rhubarb Chow-Chow.

CHAPTER 6

Breads and Flours

Manna falling from heaven. Breaking bread. I can't think of any food that's more foundational. Bread, to me, is a cultural dive. If you truly want to learn about a people, take a look at their bread: how they make it, the narrative it tells. Because it is formed from little more than flour and water, bread is as grassroots as you can get. From fry bread to focaccia to injera to pita to naan to cornbread to potato bread, it's accessible to all classes, all races, all civilizations. And as far as food culture goes, it lays the groundwork for everything that comes after, from what people drink with it to what they spread on it to what they serve alongside.

In Nana's kitchen, she was forever turning out cookies and cakes, but the pastry she was most obsessed with—pecan rolls—she always bought at the supermarket. Every morning, I'd come downstairs and there she would be, sitting with her plate of prunes and pecan rolls, sweet butter, and tea.

"You're such a great baker," nine-year-old me said to her. "Instead of going to the Acme, why don't we make pecan rolls ourselves?" And from then on, that's precisely what we'd do, and we were always stocked with our own homemade pecan rolls.

Our buttermilk biscuit recipe had been passed to Nana by her mother, Elizabeth Howard, and I can't even begin to guess how many generations it stretches back before her. Nana passed the recipe on to her daughters and of course to me, and even today, rolling out a batch of biscuits makes me feel connected to my heritage like nothing else. It's comforting to know that my hands are performing exactly the same actions as my ancestors' hands. Over the years I've changed how the biscuits are rolled out, for consistency, and I've added a brown sugar glaze. These alterations deepen the bond; it's exciting to think about what my descendants could be doing with it, twenty, sixty, or one hundred years from now.

BREAD AS LIFE

No matter the restaurant, bread is usually the first edible that's brought to the table. That's because—as I've said before—there's simply no better introduction to the foundation of a food culture. Everything else ripples out from there.

While we were taping *Top Chef* in Denver, I had the pleasure of visiting a heritage food incubator called Comal, which offers business opportunities to refugee women by allowing them to share their culinary traditions. We were taught by Syrian women to make manousheh, a type of flatbread. And while there was an obvious focus on technique, just as much of our conversation was devoted to storytelling. They spoke of the refugee camps, their struggle to get to America, and the brothers, husbands, and sons they had left behind. They spoke of the other dishes that Syrian families traditionally enjoy with this bread, and the good times they shared around the table before their worlds shattered around them.

I felt humbled to be brought into their circle in this way. Because while baguettes and biscuits, dosas and tortillas, matzo and injera all begin with flour and water, the history and narratives that are folded into the mix make them come together into so much more.

BUCKWHEAT CRACKERS

1½ cups [210 g] whole-wheat flour

1 cup [140 g] buckwheat flour

1 cup [140 g] all-purpose flour

¼ cup [35 g] sesame seeds, plus more for sprinkling

1½ tsp kosher salt

⅔ cup [160 ml] oil

Sea salt, for sprinkling

I'm sure you've heard of the chef's habit of grazing all day long in the kitchen. Not only are we too busy to sit down for full meals, but we also need to constantly quality-test everything we put out. It's a habit that's rubbed off on me at home. I could easily eat cheese, charcuterie, or crudité for dinner, because those small bites can be endlessly customized into a whole host of flavor combinations. And these crackers make a great base, especially paired with Boiled Peanut Hummus (page 86) or Spicy Pimento Cheese (page 87).

MAKES ABOUT 36 CRACKERS   Combine the flours, sesame seeds, and kosher salt in a large mixing bowl. Add the oil and 1¼ cups [300 ml] of water and mix until combined. Knead until it forms a smooth dough. Shape the dough into a ball and wrap in plastic wrap. Let sit at room temperature for 1 hour.

Preheat the oven to 350°F [180°C]. Flour a large sheet of parchment paper. Cut the dough into four pieces. Working with one piece at a time, lay it on the floured parchment paper. With a rolling pin, roll to the thickness of two sheets of paper (very thin). If it isn't absolutely as thin as you can get it, the crackers will not be crisp, but chewy.

Use a spray bottle to gently mist water over the dough. Sprinkle with sea salt and more sesame seeds. Carefully slide the dough off of the parchment paper and onto an ungreased baking sheet.

Use a pizza or pastry cutter or sharp knife to cut the dough into bite-size squares. Bake for 20 minutes or until crisp.

Remove from the oven and let cool. Eat immediately with your favorite dip or store in an airtight container for up to 1 week.

> **VARIATION**
>
> Top the rolled-out, misted cracker dough with some of the cornbread crumble from the Charred Radicchio Salad recipe (page 104).

NANA'S CORNBREAD

1 cup [140 g] all-purpose flour

1 cup [140 g] cornmeal

½ cup [100 g] sugar

1 tsp baking soda

1 tsp kosher salt

1 cup [240 ml] buttermilk

1 egg, beaten

½ cup [115 g] butter, melted

There are few staple foods that represent the Americas as directly as corn. Maize was a primary crop grown by Native Americans, which they ground into flour for multiple uses. Appalachian folks also use corn in many traditional ways, as do Southern and Northern Black folks. So of all possible breads, I'd venture cornbread is the one that speaks to the largest majority of Americans. No matter your background, everyone seems to have a family recipe that's been passed down through generations.

MAKES ONE 9 BY 13 IN [23 BY 33 CM] PAN   Preheat the oven to 350°F [180°C]. Spray a 9 by 13 in [23 by 33 cm] baking pan with nonstick cooking spray.

Mix all the dry ingredients in one large bowl, and all of the wet ingredients in another large bowl. Whisk the dry into the wet until thoroughly combined. Pour the batter into the prepared pan and bake for 20 minutes, or until a cake tester comes out clean.

Note: If you want to create a brown butter–caramelized crust, place two medium cast-iron skillets over medium-high heat. Melt 2 Tbsp of butter in each skillet. Heat until the butter gets golden brown, then pour in the cornbread batter to about halfway up the sides of each pan. Bake in the oven for 20 minutes, or until a cake tester comes out clean.

PIMENTO CHEESE SPOONBREAD

2 cups [480 ml] milk

¾ cup [105 g] cornmeal

1 cup [225 g] Spicy Pimento Cheese (page 87)

1 tsp kosher salt

2 eggs, separated

2 Tbsp butter

Adrienne Cheatham chose me to assist her in the *Top Chef* finale, and I felt absolutely honored, for many reasons. One, that she trusted me and my skills to help her win the grand prize. And two, that if she did win, she'd be the first African American woman to ever hold the title of Top Chef. I actually wept as we were plating, and that's never happened to me before, anywhere.

She wanted me to make this spoonbread for one of her courses, and afterward, I took a little container of it back to the hotel. I happened to have a little pimento cheese there too, and when I mixed the two together, this version was born.

SERVES 6   Preheat the oven to 375°F [190°C]. Butter a 2 qt [2 L] baking dish.

In a medium saucepan, combine the milk and cornmeal. Bring to a boil over medium-high heat. Lower the heat to low and cook, stirring constantly, until thick, 5 to 7 minutes. Remove from the heat.

Stir in the cheese until incorporated. Add the salt. Stir in the egg yolks, 1 at a time, and the butter.

In a separate bowl, beat the egg whites with a whisk to firm peaks (they should briefly hold their shape until falling over). Carefully fold into the cornmeal mixture. Pour into the buttered baking dish.

Bake the spoonbread for 30 to 40 minutes, or until lightly golden brown and puffed. Serve immediately while hot.

SORGHUM MOLASSES PARKER HOUSE ROLLS

2¼ tsp active dry yeast
(1 envelope)

¼ cup [60 ml] water, heated
to 100°F [35°C]

¼ cup [50 g] shortening

2 Tbsp sugar

1¾ tsp kosher salt

1 cup [240 ml] whole milk

1 egg

3½ cups [490 g] all-purpose
flour

4 Tbsp [55 g] butter, melted

Sea salt, for sprinkling

Sorghum molasses, for
drizzling

Sorghum is a cereal crop that made its way from Africa to the United States and has been widely cultivated throughout the Carolinas and the American South since the 1850s. In addition to being used as a grain, sorghum has functioned as a sugar substitute in poorer Southern regions, by being crafted into syrup or molasses.

I used to make breads daily at my restaurants, plus an extra one on Sundays, as a nod to how significant the day is to our culture. More often than not, I made these syrup-slathered rolls, and trust me when I tell you, they flew out of the kitchen. We'd have DJs spinning gospel, soul, and funk 45s, from all the way back in the 1940s and '50s, and it all worked together to create the feel-good vibe of sitting at Nana's table.

MAKES 18 ROLLS   In a mixing bowl, dissolve the yeast in the warm water. Let sit for 10 to 15 minutes, or until foamy.

In the bowl of a stand mixer (or mixing bowl), combine the shortening, sugar, and kosher salt. Whisk in the milk and egg. Add the yeast mixture and stir to combine.

Using a stand mixer fitted with a dough hook (or your hands), add the flour and stir until a dough forms. Knead until smooth and soft. Transfer to an oiled bowl, cover with a damp cloth, and let rise until doubled in size, about 1 hour.

Divide the dough into four pieces. On a floured surface, roll one dough piece into a 12 by 6 in [30.5 by 15 cm] rectangle. Brush the surface with some of the melted butter and fold the dough lengthwise. Cut the folded dough into four pieces. Butter a 9 by 13 in [23 by 33 cm] baking pan. Lay the folded rolls in the pan so they are slightly overlapping. Repeat with the remaining dough and brush the tops of the rolls with some of the melted butter. Loosely cover the rolls with a greased piece of plastic wrap. Let rise for 40 minutes.

Preheat the oven to 350°F [180°C]. Bake the rolls for 30 minutes, or until golden brown and puffed.

Brush once more with the remaining melted butter. Sprinkle with sea salt and drizzle with sorghum molasses. Serve warm.

A TOWN CALLED NICODEMUS

As I was digging deep into my family's post–Civil War journey from Virginia to Pennsylvania, I became interested in other destinations settled by freed slaves. One township that emerged during this reconstruction period was Nicodemus, in north central Kansas, where Black folks were eventually able to purchase their own land, begin their own farms, and run their own businesses.

By 1880 the city was booming, with a population of five hundred as well as a bank, a drugstore, two hotels, three churches, three general stores, an ice cream parlor, a newspaper, a baseball team, and a benefit society. All Black owned, and surrounded by cultivated land.

In response to this, the governor began finding ways to discourage Black immigrants from settling in Kansas. And in 1888, in collaboration with land commissioners of the Kansas Pacific Railroad, he built an extension of the railroad miles away from Nicodemus, leaving it stranded while surrounding cities flourished. Inevitably, businesses left, the population declined, and farm prices fell.

Now home to only twenty people, the city of Nicodemus is classified as a National Historic Landmark. And it's served as a treasure trove for people like me, intent on exploring what Black people grew and ate after coming from the motherland with nothing and emerging from slavery with nothing.

NICODEMUS BREAD

2 cups [280 g] all-purpose
flour

2 Tbsp molasses

2 tsp yeast

¼ cup [30 g] wheat germ

¼ cup [50 g] amaranth

¼ cup [35 g] sunflower seeds,
toasted

¼ cup [30 g] pine nuts,
toasted

2 cups [280 g] whole-wheat
flour

1 cup [120 g] barley flour

2 tsp kosher salt

3 eggs

¼ cup [60 ml] olive oil

1 tsp caraway seeds

1 tsp cumin seeds

1 tsp sesame seeds

1 tsp fenugreek seeds

On Facebook, I recently came across one of the only remaining restaurants in Nicodemus, a place called Ernestine's BBQ. It's open only twice a week, so I was lucky to actually be able to reach someone when I called.

The lovely woman who picked up the phone indulged me in my questions about what early settlers grew and ate; she agreed it likely revolved around corn, soy, and grains. She shared the following simple recipe, which (despite my adaptations) perfectly represents that focus. In turn, I thanked her by sharing Nana's recipe for Roly Polys (page 231). I'd like to think that on that day, we were able to further the dissemination of African American food culture, throughout generations and across continents and state lines.

MAKES ONE 13 BY 4 IN [33 BY 10 CM] LOAF   In a large bowl, combine the all-purpose flour, molasses, yeast, and 1½ cups [360 ml] of cold water. Set aside for 10 to 15 minutes, or until foamy.

Soak the wheat germ, amaranth, sunflower seeds, and pine nuts in hot water until tender, about 15 minutes. Drain in a fine-mesh strainer and set aside.

cont'd

Sift the whole-wheat flour, barley flour, and salt together into a mixing bowl. Whisk 2 of the eggs and the olive oil into the yeast mixture. Add this wet mixture to the flour mixture, along with the soaked sunflower seed mixture, and stir to combine. Knead until a dough forms.

Place the dough in a large oiled bowl. Cover with a damp cloth and let rise until doubled in size, about 1 hour.

Meanwhile, spray a 13 by 4 in [33 by 10 cm] loaf pan with cooking spray, or lightly brush with olive oil and dust with flour. In a small bowl, combine the caraway, cumin, sesame, and fenugreek seeds.

Once the dough has risen, turn it out into the loaf pan, knocking it on the table in order to pop any air bubbles. Beat the remaining egg, brush on the dough, and sprinkle with the seeds.

Preheat the oven to 350°F [180°C].

Let the dough rise for 20 minutes more, then bake for 40 minutes, or until the internal temperature reaches 190°F [90°C] or a cake tester inserted into the thickest part comes out clean.

BLACK-EYED PEA DONUTS

2¾ cups [250 g] black-eyed pea flour (available online)

2¼ tsp instant yeast (1 envelope)

3 Tbsp sugar

½ tsp kosher salt

1 cup [240 ml] milk, warmed to 100°F [35°C]

3 egg yolks

2 tsp acorn oil or hazelnut or walnut oil

4 Tbsp [55 g] butter, at room temperature

8 cups [2 L] canola oil

Spices, for dusting (optional; I like either a savory combo of black walnut powder, cumin, paprika, and kosher salt, or a sweet combo of confectioners' sugar, nutmeg, and cinnamon)

Dips, for serving (optional; try Spicy Pimento Cheese, page 87; Deviled Ham, page 88; apricot jam; or sweet potato purée)

My dear friend Joe Sasto is a magical chef. To put it in terms of music, he cooks the way Jaco Pastorius played the bass, or the way Neil Peart played the drums. So when Joe and I were asked to do a cooking demo together for the Newport Beach Wine and Food Festival, I knew I needed to come strong. I'm all about using food as a way to show connective links—to our culture and to each other. So while Joe made pasta—the dish that speaks directly to his roots—it was a pleasure standing by his side, creating savory donuts formed from peas that migrated from the African motherland to the Deep South. If you can't find acorn oil online, you can substitute hazelnut or walnut oil.

MAKES 24 DONUTS In a mixing bowl, combine 2 cups [180 g] of the flour with the yeast, sugar, and salt. Add the warm milk, egg yolks, and acorn oil and mix until smooth. Add the remaining ¾ cup [70 g] of flour and the butter and mix until it forms a soft, smooth, and still somewhat sticky dough. Cover with a damp dishcloth and let rest in a dry, warm place for 1 hour.

Fill a Dutch oven or heavy-bottomed pot with the canola oil and heat to 350°F [180°C]. Line a baking sheet with layered paper towels.

When the oil is hot, use a 1 oz [30 g] ice cream scoop or tablespoon to scoop balls of the dough into the oil, frying six at a time. Fry for 3 to 4 minutes, or until the donuts are brown and cooked through.

Using a slotted spoon, transfer the donuts to the prepared baking sheet. Dust with spices. Repeat with the remaining dough and serve with dips of your choice.

SPAETZLE

2 cups [280 g] all-purpose flour

7 eggs, beaten

¼ cup [60 ml] milk

2 tsp ground nutmeg

1 tsp onion powder

Kosher salt and freshly cracked black pepper

Spaetzle is basically a type of pasta with German/Hungarian roots. Once it was boiled, Nana would simply toss her spaetzle with brown butter and parsley. But they take well to just about any preparation (try making them into mac and cheese) and are ideal for rounding out any meal; serve with whatever meat, fish, vegetable, or broth-based dish you'd like.

SERVES 6 Combine the flour, eggs, milk, nutmeg, and onion powder in a mixing bowl. Season with salt and pepper. Cover with plastic wrap and refrigerate for 1 hour.

Bring a large pot of water to a boil. Set a colander on top; it should fit firmly on top without touching the water. Fill a bowl with salted ice water and set aside.

When the water is boiling, turn the heat down to medium. Being careful of any rising steam (you can wear oven mitts while you do this), pour the spaetzle batter into the colander, forcing it through the holes with a rubber spatula. Work as quickly as you can, as the rising steam will start to cook whatever batter remains in the colander.

When all the batter is in the water, remove the colander and stir the floating spaetzle to keep it from clumping. Cook for 3 to 4 minutes. With a slotted spoon or spider, transfer the spaetzle directly into the ice bath. When cooled, either toss in a bowl with a tiny bit of olive oil or lay out on a baking sheet without oil—either method keeps the spaetzle from sticking together. From this point, you can cover the spaetzle in plastic and refrigerate for up to 2 days, or cook it immediately in your favorite sauce.

> **SWITCH UP YOUR SPAETZLE**
>
> I've played around with a variety of wheats when making spaetzle, from sorghum to buckwheat flour. In addition to contributing unique flavor, they also offer a great depth and heartiness not necessarily achieved with white flour. The buckwheat, for example, showcases spaetzle's Germanic roots, and it's terrific with braised meat, cabbage, and a nice dark beer.

BROWN SUGAR BUTTERMILK BISCUITS

2 cups [280 g] all-purpose flour

2 cups [240 g] cake flour

6 Tbsp [75 g] baking powder

1 Tbsp kosher salt

1 cup [340 g] honey

1 cup [226 g] cold butter, shredded on the coarse side of a box grater or chopped

1¼ cups [300 ml] buttermilk

¼ cup [55 g] unsalted butter, melted

3 Tbsp packed brown sugar

The first time I ever had these biscuits was at my Aunt Sara Mae's house. But I found out later on that the recipe wasn't hers: It was one that my great-grandmother Elizabeth Howard passed down to Nana Browne and then to her children. So while biscuits may seem like a simple thing, they speak directly to my heritage. And when I prepare them, I imagine all the hands that made them before me.

However this recipe originally came into being—whether Elizabeth was the creator, or someone before her—it makes me happy to know I'm keeping a family tradition alive, many generations later. And it brings me even greater joy to share this recipe with the world. It's like I'm opening my heart or extending my hand in friendship. I've often said that bread is love. And these buttermilk biscuits are the embodiment of that.

MAKES ABOUT 36 BISCUITS Preheat the oven to 325°F [165°C].

In a large bowl, combine the flours, baking powder, and salt (don't bother to sift them). Mix until thoroughly combined. Add the honey and shredded butter. Mix by hand until all the butter is incorporated into the flour; it should have a sand-like texture. Add the buttermilk, make your hand into a claw, and stir in the buttermilk to form a wet dough with a gummy consistency, being careful not to overmix. Dust the top of the dough lightly with flour.

cont'd

Dust your hands and a work surface well with flour. Using your hands, roll the biscuits into 2 oz [55 g] balls. Arrange in rows on a baking pan, about 1 in [2.5 cm] apart.

Bake for 20 minutes, then rotate the pan and bake for 20 to 30 minutes more. To test for doneness, lightly tap the tops of the biscuits in the center of the tray. If the impression of your finger remains, the dough is still raw. If the tops spring back when tapped, the biscuits are done. Transfer to a cooling rack.

In a small bowl, combine the melted butter and brown sugar. Using a pastry brush, spread the mixture over the tops of the biscuits. Return to the oven until the sugar just melts and gets sticky, about 5 minutes. Remove from the oven and serve immediately.

BUCKWHEAT AND RYE DUMPLINGS

2 cups [480 g] ricotta cheese

¼ cup [25 g] grated Parmesan cheese

4 egg yolks

1 tsp kosher salt

1 tsp freshly cracked black pepper

½ tsp ground allspice

1 cup [140 g] all-purpose flour

1 cup [140 g] buckwheat flour

Rye flour, for dusting

Dumplings are integral to Amish cooking, found in all manner of soups and stews. But I also like letting them be the star by making them with hearty, earthy flours that allow them to stand up to bold meats. Try these with braised brisket or roasted lamb or goat, or use the bones to form a soup, then float some dumplings on top.

SERVES 4   In a bowl, whisk together the cheeses, egg yolks, salt, pepper, and allspice until smooth. Add the flours and mix until a firm dough forms.

Dust a work surface lightly with rye flour. Roll out the dough into a ½ in [12 mm] thick rope. Cut into ¼ in [6 mm] cubes.

Bring a pot of salted water to a rolling boil. Add the dumplings and gently poach for 3 to 4 minutes. Strain, using a spider or colander, and let cool on a baking sheet.

Serve as desired (seared in brown butter or placed in soup are two of my favorite preparations). They will keep, refrigerated in an airtight container, for up to 2 days.

RED VELVET CORNMEAL MADELEINES

1 cup [140 g] all-purpose flour

1 cup [140 g] cornmeal

1 cup [240 ml] buttermilk

2 eggs

⅓ cup [80 ml] bacon fat or blended oil

1 Tbsp red food coloring

¼ cup [50 g] sugar

2 Tbsp unsweetened cocoa powder

1 Tbsp plus 1 tsp baking powder

½ tsp kosher salt

Besides Crispy Potato Waffles (page 69), these are my go-to vehicles for chicken liver mousse (see page 188). Drizzle with a little aged balsamic, and you've got the perfect, colorful, bite-size canapé, paired with some sparkling wine or (my preference) Cheerwine, that famous soda pop from the South.

MAKES 24 MADELEINES   Preheat the oven to 350°F [180°C].

Put all the ingredients in a mixing bowl and stir until combined.

Spray two madeleine trays with nonstick cooking spray and fill the molds with batter (if you have only one tray, you can work in batches). Place the madeleine tray(s) on baking sheets and bake for 10 minutes. Let cool. Gently tap out the madeleines, and repeat the process if necessary.

Enjoy as is, or spread with chicken liver mousse or Spicy Pimento Cheese (page 87).

PECAN ROLLS

FOR THE DOUGH

1 cup [240 ml] milk, heated to 100°F [35°C]

⅓ cup [65 g] granulated sugar

1 tsp active dry yeast

2 large eggs

1 cup [140 g] all-purpose flour, leveled

1 tsp kosher salt

½ cup [113 g] butter, cut into thirds, at room temperature

FOR THE CARAMEL SAUCE

¾ cup [170 g] butter

1½ cups [300 g] packed brown sugar

⅓ cup [115 g] honey

⅓ cup [80 ml] cream

1 tsp kosher salt

FOR THE FILLING

2 cups [240 g] chopped, toasted pecans

⅓ cup [65 g] granulated sugar

⅓ cup [65 g] packed brown sugar

1 tsp ground cinnamon

½ tsp ground nutmeg

½ tsp ground allspice

½ tsp kosher salt

The same way that I'm known for my biscuits, Nana was known for her pecan rolls. There was never a moment that these rolls weren't in her house. On the regular, our place smelled like caramel and cinnamon, and at least once a day you'd find Nana sitting alone, maybe humming a hymn, enjoying a pecan roll with prune butter and a cup of hot tea.

So if you ever want to channel Nana Browne's vibe, make a batch of these rolls and then sit on the porch watching the sun come up. You're guaranteed to achieve Zen.

MAKES 12 ROLLS   *To make the dough:* Combine the warm milk, granulated sugar, and yeast in a mixing bowl. Stir until combined, then let sit for about 5 minutes, or until you see bubbles and foam.

Note: It's essential to have the milk at the right temperature. If it's too hot, the heat will kill the yeast. If you don't see any bubbles, you'll need to try again.

Once bubbles form, add the eggs and whisk until smooth. Set aside. In a separate large bowl, combine the flour and salt. Slowly add the egg and yeast mixture and stir until combined, scraping down the sides of the bowl.

cont'd

While stirring, add the three pieces of butter, making sure each chunk is totally incorporated before adding the next. Keep stirring for 3 to 4 minutes, until it forms a smooth, sticky dough.

Form the dough into a loose ball and put into a greased mixing bowl. Cover with a damp cloth and chill in the refrigerator for 2 hours.

To make the caramel sauce: Melt the butter in a small saucepan. Remove the pan from the heat and add the brown sugar, honey, cream, and salt, and ⅓ cup [80 ml] of water. Whisk until smooth, and let cool to room temperature.

To make the filling: Combine the pecans, both sugars, spices, and salt in a mixing bowl.

To make the rolls: Preheat the oven to 350°F [180°C]. Bring a teakettle full of water to a boil, then pour the water into a 9 by 13 in [23 by 33 cm] baking pan. Place the pan on the bottom rack of the oven with another rack on top, and heat for 5 minutes. Turn off the oven.

Pour the caramel sauce over the bottom of another 9 by 13 in [23 by 33 cm] baking pan, making sure it's totally covered. Set aside.

Dust a work surface with flour. Transfer the dough to the surface and knead it a couple of times to make it workable. Using a rolling pin, roll the dough into a large rectangle, about 12 by 18 in [30.5 by 46 cm] and ¼ in [6 mm] thick. Sprinkle the pecan filling evenly over the dough.

Starting at the long edge, begin rolling up the dough. As you're rolling, occasionally run your hands down the dough from the center to the edges, so it stays evenly proportioned throughout.

Seal the roll by crimping and pinching the seam. Using a serrated knife dipped in flour, cut the roll into 12 even slices, and place the slices, spiral-side up, on the caramel.

Cover the rolls with a greased sheet of plastic wrap. Place the pan in the (turned off) oven, nested in the pan of water on the lowest rack, with the other rack on top. Let rise for 45 minutes, or until doubled in size.

After 45 minutes, remove the pan of rolls and the pan of water, and preheat the oven to 350°F [180°C]. Place the pan of rolls (not the pan of water) back in the oven, and bake for about 40 minutes, or until golden.

Remove the pan of rolls from the oven and cool on a rack for 15 minutes. Invert a platter on the top and, gripping the sides together, invert the two so the rolls drop onto the platter and the caramel oozes all over. Serve immediately, bottom-side up, or cover and store, unrefrigerated, for up to 2 days.

CHAPTER 7

Shugga's

Desserts are a huge part of Amish culture. Every single Amish-run diner sells sticky-sweet shoofly pie, shoofly tarts, and shoofly munchkins (basically balls of molasses rolled in crumb crust), and every single store has shelves stacked high with whoopie pies, coconut cream pies, donuts, sweet breads, and cakes. And as you can tell by Nana's desire for sweet coffee and sweeter tea, along with prunes and pecan rolls spread with sweet butter, she had a serious sweet tooth. Which of course got passed down to me.

Whenever Nana made her chocolate mousse with a graham cracker crust for company, she'd have to ensure it stayed untouched—by making another one for the house. But it wasn't just the desserts themselves I fell in love with. I developed just as much of a passion for the process. The fact that it was measured and precise—so different from the otherwise freestyle approach in Amish soul food cooking—gave me structure and comfort. I appreciated the care and technique that went into producing the best baked delight you could with whatever you had on hand. Which was usually the homeliest of ingredients, such as flour and eggs for funnel cake, or sweet potatoes for pie.

But perhaps the greatest reason that desserts hold such a special place in my heart is that I have actual recipes handwritten by Nana, for Roly Polys (Apple Dumplings, page 231), apple crisps, and more. When it comes to replicating other dishes of hers, it's more of a conversation between me and my aunts—they channel as much as they can remember into words. Whereas with so many of Nana's sweets, I have actual written records from her. Sort of like a collection of love letters.

NANA BROWNE'S ROLY POLYS (APPLE DUMPLINGS)

FOR THE PASTRY

1½ cups [310 g] shortening, preferably Crisco, packed

½ cup [120 ml] boiling water, plus more if needed

¼ cup [60 ml] milk

4½ cups [630 g] all-purpose flour

1 Tbsp granulated sugar

2 tsp kosher salt

FOR THE FILLING

4 tart baking apples, preferably Granny Smith, peeled, cored, and diced

½ cup [100 g] packed brown sugar

6 Tbsp [90 g] granulated sugar, plus more for sprinkling

2 tsp ground cinnamon

2 tsp kosher salt

½ tsp ground ginger

½ tsp ground nutmeg

2 Tbsp butter

FOR THE CUSTARD SAUCE

½ cup [100 g] granulated sugar

1 Tbsp cornstarch

3 Tbsp butter

2 cups [480 ml] heavy cream

¼ cup [60 ml] white rum

2 tsp vanilla extract

The elders in my family still go crazy over this roly poly—a.k.a. apple dumpling—recipe. It's pretty touching listening to a bunch of old folks reminiscing about a dessert Nana made for them when they were young. This just goes to show the power of food to create lasting memories—to transport you back in time, at any age.

This was Nana's go-to dessert to serve her kids, and they passed it down to us. Whenever one of my aunts prepared a batch of roly polys, they'd put out a family-wide call, and we'd pile right into our cars and head on over. They're that good.

Considering the clear Pennsylvania Dutch influence of apple dumplings, it's hard not to wonder about the true origins of roly polys in my family. Were they truly passed down from my great-grandmother? Having Nana's handwritten recipe makes them a real heirloom. And the fact that they call for hot water pastry—made with Spry shortening, no less (the company is long defunct)—is a testament to the age of this recipe!

MAKES 4   *To make the pastry:* In a mixing bowl, combine the shortening, boiling water, and milk. Whisk the mixture until smooth and thick.

cont'd

In another medium bowl, sift together the flour, granulated sugar, and salt. Add the flour mixture to the shortening mixture and combine with a wooden spoon until a dough starts to form. Lightly knead the mixture with your hands until the consistency is even, adding more boiling water, if needed, to create a smooth dough.

Divide the dough into four evenly sized pieces. On a lightly floured work surface, use a rolling pin to flatten each piece into an oval or rectangle about ¼ in [6 mm] thick and roughly 6 by 10 in [15 by 25 cm]. Wrap each sheet of dough with plastic and refrigerate for 30 minutes.

While the dough rests, make the filling: In a bowl, combine the apples, both sugars, cinnamon, salt, ginger, and nutmeg. Set aside until the apples begin to release liquid, about 15 minutes. Using a slotted spoon, transfer the apples from the liquid into a medium bowl. Reserve both the apples and the liquid.

Preheat the oven to 350°F [180°C].

Place the dough rectangles on a flat surface. Evenly divide the apple mixture among the four pieces of dough, making sure to leave about 1 in [2.5 cm] of bare dough on all sides. Divide the butter among the four pieces, dotting each with ½ Tbsp. Sprinkle sugar on each. Fold the dough up and over the apples and pinch it together to seal the apples inside of the dough completely (you can moisten the edges with water if needed to stick). Place on an ungreased baking sheet, seal-side down. Bake until lightly golden, about 30 minutes.

Meanwhile, in a small saucepan over low heat, reduce the reserved apple liquid until slightly syrupy, about 5 minutes. After the roly polys have baked for 30 minutes, brush the tops with this glaze and return them to the oven until the pastry is browned and the glaze is shiny, 15 minutes more. Remove to a cooling rack and let cool while you make the custard sauce.

To make the custard sauce: In a small dish, combine the granulated sugar and cornstarch. In a small saucepan, melt the butter. Add the heavy cream and the cornstarch mixture, whisking over low heat until the sauce begins to thicken, about 5 minutes. Remove from the heat and add the rum and vanilla. Stir until combined.

To serve, place each roly poly in a bowl or on a rimmed plate and spoon the custard sauce over the top.

WHOOPIE PIES

FOR THE CAKES

1¾ cups [245 g] all-purpose flour

⅔ cup [50 g] cocoa powder

1 tsp baking powder

½ tsp kosher salt

¼ tsp baking soda

1 egg

½ cup [120 ml] buttermilk

¼ cup [60 ml] vanilla syrup (store-bought or homemade simple syrup)

1 Tbsp instant coffee

1 cup [200 g] sugar

¾ cup [170 g] butter, at room temperature

FOR THE FILLING

5 egg whites

1⅔ cups [330 g] sugar

¼ tsp kosher salt

2 cups [452 g] butter, at room temperature

2 Tbsp marshmallow crème

1 tsp vanilla extract

As kids, we got to enjoy this treat as often as three times a week. If you visited any of the Amish markets, you absolutely didn't leave without picking one up to eat on your walk or drive home. Seeing a person carrying a whoopie pie in my neck of the woods was as common as seeing someone in France carrying a baguette.

MAKES 8 PIES   Preheat the oven to 375°F [190°C]. Line a baking sheet with parchment paper.

To make the cakes: In a large bowl, combine the flour, cocoa, baking powder, salt, and baking soda. In a separate bowl, whisk together the egg, buttermilk, vanilla syrup, and instant coffee until combined. In a stand mixer or with a handheld mixer, cream the sugar and butter together until fluffy.

With the mixer on low speed, slowly add first the flour mixture to the butter mixture, then the egg mixture, and thoroughly combine. Remove the bowl from the mixer and scrape the bottom of the bowl with a rubber spatula to make sure there aren't unmixed patches of flour or butter.

cont'd

Using a small ice cream scoop, portion out sixteen evenly sized scoops of batter (about 2 oz [55 g] each) and place them at least 2 in [5 cm] apart on the prepared baking sheet. Bake for 8 to 10 minutes, then remove from the oven and set aside to cool.

To make the filling: In the bottom pan of a double boiler (see sidebar, page 245), bring water to a simmer. In a mixing bowl, whip the egg whites, sugar, and salt for about 1 minute, or until foamy but not stiff. Place the bowl over the simmering double boiler and whisk constantly until the egg whites reach 160°F [70°C]. This technique will melt the sugar.

Transfer the mixture to a stand mixer, or use an electric hand mixer to whip on high speed until the mixture forms firm peaks (they should briefly hold their shape until falling over). Let cool to room temperature.

Once the egg white mixture has cooled, using a paddle attachment on low speed, fold in the butter, marshmallow crème, and vanilla. Transfer to a pastry bag. Pipe a 1 in [2.5 cm] thick layer of filling over the flat side of eight of the cakes, and sandwich with the other eight cakes. Serve. Store leftover pies in an airtight container at room temperature for up to 3 days.

Note: This recipe will likely yield more filling than you need, but having excess vanilla crème around is never a problem. We like to use it as a dip for pretzel rods or a topping for cola floats. The crème will last for up to 1 week, refrigerated in an airtight container.

IN A BAKING STATE OF MIND

I've likened the difference between savory cooking and sweet baking to that between jazz and classical music. When it comes to jazz, you can add and subtract and improvise and tweak things to get a piece back on track. Even if a musician is out of tune or can't keep up, you can manipulate the sound to make things right again. Whereas with classical, you have to follow the rules. You have to stay on course. You have to put all your attention into perfectly playing or singing your part. And if you don't, it can't be made right again. Like classical music, baking, as an art, is extremely precise.

I think that's why I'm never more at peace than when I'm making a pie or rolling out a batch of biscuits. Because it puts me right back in the mindset of how things were back then with Nana. We had time for those biscuits. We had time for each other. And finding that time would have been a struggle if I had grown up with my own parents, the same way it is with my own family today. I'm sure our children feel the pull of having so much on our plates. Why can't you give me 100 percent of your time? Why do you have to worry about the restaurant, or paying this bill, when I'm standing right in front of you?

But my grandparents didn't have any of that. I was the most important thing on their plate. So it was, let's go fishing and just fish. Let's go for a walk and just walk. Let's bake these cookies and that's all we're going to do: bake.

Although I was the only child in the house, I was surrounded by family in tiny Coatesville, as my aunts and uncles and cousins lived only blocks away. Nana had raised everyone up in the church as Jehovah's Witnesses, which meant we didn't recognize holidays or birthdays. But as I got older, and people started leaving the church, they found more opportunity to come together and celebrate. And rather than risk separation from her family, Nana would join in.

And so, the connection I shared with my grandmother in the kitchen began to extend to my aunts. We'd go for Thanksgiving at Aunt Sara Mae's house, or Christmas at Aunt Mim's, or a birthday at Aunt Shirley's. And I'd discover they made dishes that were recognizably Nana's, but done in their own way, evolved for their own families. Being very familiar with Nana's repertoire, and understandably loyal to it, I was shocked at first. But I came to love and appreciate their versions too and realized that rather than being an affront, they were a way of honoring her . . . of taking what she'd taught them and making it their own.

Those kitchen gatherings also became the way I learned about my family. They'd group around the stove and us kids would eavesdrop, listening to them talk about this cousin who'd cut school, or another who'd left home. So whether it was gossiping or grieving, or laughing or crying, cooking became the backdrop. We just happened to be in the kitchen when everything—when life itself—was going down.

GERMAN CHOCOLATE DONUTS

FOR THE DONUTS

3¾ cups [525 g] all-purpose flour

½ cup [40 g] cocoa powder

1 Tbsp plus 1 tsp baking powder

1 Tbsp kosher salt

¾ tsp instant coffee

1¼ cups plus 2 Tbsp [280 g] granulated sugar

3 Tbsp butter, at room temperature

5 egg yolks

1¾ cups [420 g] sour cream

Canola oil, for frying

Confectioners' sugar, for dusting

FOR THE SAUCE

1 cup [200 g] packed brown sugar

½ cup [113 g] butter

1 cup [240 ml] evaporated milk

3 egg yolks

2 cups [200 g] sweetened shredded coconut

1 cup [120 g] toasted chopped pecans

1 tsp vanilla extract

My mother passed away the day before I got married, and she got the chance to see only one of her four grandchildren: my daughter Elena, once, when she was three years old. They clicked right after Elena took a spill in the playground. My mother picked her up, brushed off her knees, said something funny, and was able to get a chuckle out of her. I knew then that she had the potential of being a wonderful grandmother. But that never came to pass.

I often think about her and wonder if we could have continued to heal from the harsh past that we shared. If she were allowed to leave heaven for ten minutes, my guess is that she would probably share the first nine with her grandchildren, and the last minute telling me how to get my ass right.

Every now and then, I'll catch inspiration remembering my mother. These donuts sprang from her all-time favorite dessert: Sara Lee brand German chocolate cake. So whenever I fantasize about having my mother back, it now includes her enjoying these donuts, while reading me the riot act.

cont'd

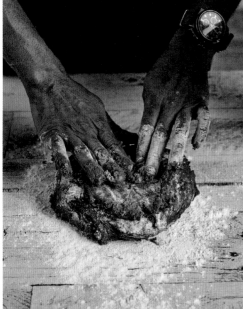

MAKES 12 DONUTS   *To make the donuts:* In a large mixing bowl, sift together the flour, cocoa, baking powder, salt, and instant coffee. In the bowl of a stand mixer fitted with the paddle attachment, beat the granulated sugar, butter, and egg yolks on high speed until fluffy, about 3 minutes.

Lower the speed to medium, and fold in the sour cream. Lower the speed to low and slowly add the flour mixture, about 2 Tbsp at a time, making sure each addition is totally incorporated before adding more flour. Don't overmix: This will make the donuts tough.

Coat a sheet of plastic wrap with nonstick cooking spray to cover the dough and refrigerate for 1 hour.

Lightly flour a work surface. Line a baking sheet with parchment paper and spray it with nonstick cooking spray. Turn out the chilled dough (which will be rather sticky and tacky) onto the floured surface and use a floured rolling pin to roll to ½ in [12 mm] thickness. Dip a 3 in [7.5 cm] round cookie cutter in flour and use to cut twelve circles from the dough. Dip a 1½ in [4 cm] round cookie cutter in flour and use to cut out the centers. Use a spatula to transfer the donuts to the prepared sheet. Refrigerate for 20 minutes.

In a large Dutch oven or heavy-bottomed pot, heat the canola oil to 350°F [180°C]. Use a candy or digital thermometer to monitor the heat. Line plates with paper towels to drain the fried donuts.

Working in batches so as to not overcrowd the pot, gently lift the donuts with a spatula and lower into the hot oil. Fry on each side for about 2½ minutes, or until crispy. Make sure to monitor the oil in between batches to maintain the temperature. Use a slotted spoon to transfer to the paper towels and dust immediately with confectioners' sugar.

To make the sauce: In a medium saucepan, combine the brown sugar, butter, evaporated milk, and egg yolks. Bring to a soft boil over medium heat, whisking occasionally. Once the mixture boils, whisk continuously for about 5 minutes as the sauce thickens.

Remove from the heat and stir in the coconut, pecans, and vanilla. Let cool slightly and spoon over the donuts. The sauce will continue to thicken and get stiffer as it cools, so work quickly. Serve warm (and messy!) or let cool to set completely.

BUTTERSCOTCH "KRIMPETS" (MAPLE LOG DONUTS)

FOR THE CAKE

1 Tbsp dry yeast

1 cup [240 ml] water, heated to 100°F [35°C]

1 Tbsp plus ½ cup [100 g] granulated sugar

4 cups [560 g] all-purpose flour

2 tsp kosher salt

½ tsp baking powder

¼ cup [50 g] shortening

3 egg yolks

½ tsp vanilla extract

Canola oil, for frying

FOR THE ICING

1 lb [455 g] confectioners' sugar

⅓ cup [80 ml] hot water

1½ tsp corn syrup

1 tsp maple extract

¼ tsp kosher salt

¼ tsp vanilla extract

If you grew up in Southeastern Pennsylvania—or the Delaware Valley, as they call it—then you definitely know about the TastyKakes made by the Tasty Baking Company. It's basically our Hostess or Entenmann's. Kids' lunch boxes would invariably be packed with Frosty Kandy Kakes, Iced Fudge Cookie Bars, Tasty Klair Baked Pies, Swirly Cupkakes, and the big daddy of them all: Butterscotch Krimpets. Seriously, these pastries are as important to PA as cheesesteaks, soft pretzels, and the Philadelphia Eagles. I've even heard stories of people being buried with boxes of Krimpets in their caskets.

Though the Krimpet is more of a sponge cake, I have reimagined the famous regional treat as a kind of donut, which are huge in the Amish community. Donuts even have a holiday named after them: Fastnacht Day (the Pennsylvania Dutch counterpart to Mardi Gras or Fat Tuesday). I'd venture to say this recipe is tasty enough to plan an entire celebration around!

MAKES 12 DONUTS   *To make the cake:* In a mixing bowl, combine the yeast, water, and 1 Tbsp of the granulated sugar and let sit for 5 to 8 minutes, until frothy. In another large bowl, sift together the flour, the remaining ½ cup [100 g] of granulated sugar, the salt, and baking powder.

When the yeast is foamy, add the shortening, egg yolks, and vanilla to the bowl and whisk to combine. Add this mixture to the bowl of sifted dry ingredients and combine until a smooth dough forms.

Grease a large cutting board (about 18 by 24 in [46 by 61 cm]) and a large sheet of plastic wrap. Put the dough on the board and cover it loosely with the wrap. Let rise at room temperature for 1 hour.

After 1 hour, punch down the dough and lightly flour a work surface. Roll out the dough into a rectangle the approximate size of the cutting board. Trim the edges, then cut into twelve evenly sized rectangles. Cover again with the greased plastic wrap, and let rise for 30 minutes more.

Fill a Dutch oven or heavy-bottomed pot half full with canola oil. Line a tray with paper towels to drain the donuts. Heat the oil to 350°F [180°C]. Monitor the temperature with a candy or digital thermometer. Gently lower two donuts at a time into the oil and fry for 40 seconds on each side, or until golden. Using a slotted spoon, carefully transfer the donuts to the paper towels. Repeat with the remaining donuts. Let cool to room temperature.

To make the icing: Add all the ingredients to a small saucepan and bring to a boil over high heat. Lower to a simmer and cook, stirring, for 5 minutes. Remove from the heat and let cool for 10 minutes.

Glaze the tops of the donuts with the icing and let set at room temperature. Once set, enjoy right away!

SILKY CHOCOLATE MOUSSE WITH COCOA CRUNCH

2 cups [360 g] chocolate chips

¾ cup [170 g] butter

¾ cup [150 g] sugar

6 eggs

Cocoa Krispies (or your favorite crunchy, sweetened cereal), for serving

This was one of the very first desserts I learned to make as a professional chef. It's super dense and really hits the spot if you're a chocolate freak. Adding a crunchy element is a great textural contrast to the silky smoothness of the mousse. I've played around with everything from hazelnut brown sugar crumble to blackberry Pop Rocks, but this version was Nana's favorite. It was inspired by the time I made it for her when she was babysitting my second cousins, and they started mixing their chocolate cereal into the mousse.

MAKES 4 CUPS [946 ML]   Melt the chocolate and butter over a double boiler (see sidebar).

Using a stand mixer or handheld mixer, whip together the sugar and eggs to the ribbon stage (very smooth and thick). Slowly pour the chocolate mixture into the egg mixture and gently fold together until completely incorporated (no streaks).

Transfer the mousse into whatever vessels you prefer, such as demitasse cups, small soufflé cups, teacups, small clamp jars, or even a cake pan.

Refrigerate for 12 hours or until set. Top with Cocoa Krispies and serve. Store leftover mousse, covered, in the refrigerator for up to 2 days.

HOW TO MAKE A DOUBLE BOILER

If you're melting chocolate, making a custard base for ice cream, or warming up something that needs a delicate touch, using a double boiler is a foolproof way to go about it. And you can assemble one with kitchen equipment you probably already have.

Select a saucepan and a metal mixing bowl that will fit snugly into the pan, with at least 1 in [2.5 cm] of clearance from the hot water. Bring 1 in [2.5 cm] of water to a very low simmer in the pan. Put the ingredients to be heated or melted in the bowl, and nest it in the pan.

AUNT SARA MAE'S BUTTERMILK CAKE

FOR THE CAKE

1 cup [200 g] granulated sugar

½ cup [113 g] butter, at room temperature

2 eggs

2 cups [280 g] all-purpose flour

1 Tbsp baking powder

1 tsp kosher salt

1¼ cups [300 ml] buttermilk

2 tsp vanilla extract

FOR THE ICING

1 cup [226 g] butter, at room temperature

4 cups [480 g] confectioners' sugar

2 tsp buttermilk

1 tsp vanilla extract

When you were going over to Aunt Sara Mae's house, you knew you were going to eat well. Her baking skills were incredible. For a while, she was the one who would make all the birthday cakes for the family, and she even started the tradition that on your special day, the very first meal you eat is cake.

This is in the top three of my all-time favorite Aunt Sara Mae creations. We'd even run this during our Sunday gospel suppers at Butterfunk Kitchen, and of course, it was a hit.

MAKES ONE 15 BY 11 IN [38 BY 28 CM] SHEET CAKE Preheat the oven to 375°F [190°C]. Line a 15 by 11 in [38 by 28 cm] baking pan with parchment paper and grease the paper.

To make the cake: In a stand mixer, cream together the granulated sugar and butter. When fluffy, add the eggs and stir until just combined. In a large bowl, combine the flour, baking powder, and salt, then gradually add to the mixture in the mixer. Fold in the buttermilk and vanilla.

Pour the batter into the prepared pan. Bake for 25 minutes, or until a toothpick inserted in the center comes out clean. Carefully remove from the pan and the parchment and transfer to a serving platter. Let cool at room temperature.

To make the icing: Add the butter to a (clean) stand mixer fitted with the paddle attachment and whip until fluffy. Add the confectioners' sugar, 1 cup [120 g] at a time, and whip at medium speed. Once all the sugar is incorporated, add the buttermilk and vanilla and whip until fluffy. Spread evenly over the cake top and sides.

BUTTERMILK CORNBREAD ICE CREAM

¾ cup [180 ml] heavy cream

1 Tbsp cornstarch

⅓ cup [65 g] sugar

1 Tbsp corn syrup

¼ cup [60 g] cream cheese, at room temperature

⅛ tsp kosher salt

2 cups [480 ml] buttermilk

2½ cups [570 g] cornbread cubes (use Nana's Cornbread recipe on page 205 or store-bought)

½ cup [170 g] honey, sorghum, or Yam Molasses (page 46)

Anyone who knows me personally knows that ice cream is my weakness. Even as a young cook, it was my favorite medium for experimenting with flavors, from fresh bay leaf to eucalyptus syrup. So it only stood to reason that eventually I'd use it to incorporate the flavors of my childhood and my hometown.

As far as this recipe is concerned, it's yet another way to deal with the "problem" of leftover cornbread: creating a velvety smooth ice cream with natural sweetness from corn, juxtaposed with a slight acidity offered by buttermilk. As for the recipe on page 249, well, no sweet speaks to Coatesville, PA, in quite the same way as shoofly pie.

MAKES ABOUT 1 QT [960 ML] In a small bowl, make a slurry with 2 Tbsp of the heavy cream and the cornstarch.

In a saucepan, whisk together the remaining 10 Tbsp [150 ml] of heavy cream with the sugar and corn syrup and bring to a boil. Gradually whisk in the cornstarch slurry and cook for 30 seconds, or until slightly thickened. Remove from the heat.

In a stand mixer, beat together the cream cheese and salt. Gradually beat the warm heavy cream into the cream cheese, then add the buttermilk.

Add 1½ cups [340 g] of the cornbread cubes to a large bowl and pour the cream cheese mixture over the top. Let sit at room temperature for 30 minutes.

cont'd

After 30 minutes, strain the mixture through a fine-mesh strainer and into a bowl, pushing any remaining cornbread crumbs through the strainer. Refrigerate for 12 hours.

After 12 hours, add this custard to an ice cream machine and churn, following the manufacturer's directions. Transfer the ice cream to a prechilled, freezer-safe container and freeze for at least 4 hours.

Meanwhile, preheat the oven to 375°F [190°C]. Spread the remaining 1 cup [230 g] of cornbread cubes on a rimmed baking sheet and bake until just warm, about 5 minutes. Toss with the honey or molasses and bake until golden and sticky but not burnt. Let cool to room temperature.

To serve, top scoops of ice cream with the cornbread crumble.

SHOOFLY PIE ICE CREAM

FOR THE CUSTARD

1 cup [240 ml] whole milk

1 cup [240 ml] heavy cream

¾ cup [150 g] sugar

2 Tbsp molasses, plus more for serving

4 egg yolks

1 tsp kosher salt

1 tsp vanilla extract

FOR THE TOPPING

1 cup [140 g] all-purpose flour

1 cup [200 g] sugar

½ tsp baking soda

1 egg, beaten

4 Tbsp [55 g] butter, melted

How are you gonna have an Amish-influenced cookbook without a mention of shoofly pie?

Developed by the Pennsylvania Dutch, the molasses-based, crumb-topped pie can be found in diners and bakeries throughout Amish-settled communities and beyond. There's the "dry bottom" variety, which has more of a cakelike texture. But just like the pesky, sugar-seeking insects for which it presumably got its name, true shoofly enthusiasts are invariably drawn to the "wet bottom" versions of the pie. This involves adding water and a little corn syrup to your molasses mix and baking it for a slightly shorter time than you otherwise would. When it cools, it develops a moist and fudgy lower layer that's sweet, syrupy, and indescribably delicious. This is the rendition I've always made, and the one that inspired this ice cream. Although instead of a wet bottom, it has a sticky top!

If you're a shoofly skeptic, I'm convinced this ice cream frees it from the "acquired taste" category. And for me, it still manages to evoke memories of the state fair, hayrides, and catching lightning bugs under the Pennsylvania Amish Country moonlight. *Note:* You'll need to start this ice cream a day ahead.

MAKES ABOUT 1 QT [960 ML]   *To make the custard:* In a saucepan, combine the milk, cream, sugar, and molasses. Heat over medium-low heat, stirring constantly, until it just comes to a simmer.

In a mixing bowl, whisk together the egg yolks and salt. Take about 2 Tbsp of the hot cream and whisk it into the egg yolks, stirring constantly so they don't curdle. (This is called tempering the yolks.)

cont'd

Slowly stream the egg mixture into the cream mixture on the stove and whisk constantly over low heat until it's thick enough to cling to the back of a spoon, about 5 minutes. Remove from the heat and strain through a colander into a bowl. Let the bowl of custard come to room temperature, then stir in the vanilla. Cover the top with plastic wrap and refrigerate overnight.

The next day, churn the custard in an ice cream machine, following the manufacturer's instructions. Transfer the ice cream to a prechilled, freezer-safe container, cover, and freeze for at least 4 hours.

To make the topping: Preheat the oven to 350°F [180°C]. Line a rimmed baking sheet with parchment paper.

Sift the flour, sugar, and baking soda into a bowl. Add the egg and butter and fold everything together until pebble-size crumbs of dough are formed. Do not work into a dough ball. Transfer the crumbs to the prepared baking sheet and bake for 20 minutes. Remove from the oven and let cool and dry out at room temperature.

To serve, top scoops of ice cream with the shoofly crumbs and a drizzle of molasses.

MISS MOLLY'S ICEBERGS

6 cups [1.4 L] cubed, seeded watermelon, or an equivalent amount of any fruit or juice

Six 8 oz [236 ml] Dixie cups

6 ice-pop sticks

There was a very nice old lady called Miss Molly, who lived on the corner of Tenth Avenue and Merchant Street, in our East End neighborhood of Coatesville. Nana used to say she was her cousin, and that may have been the truth, but in general, Black folks who are very close will always refer to each other as cousins.

Anyway, Miss Molly had a little hustle going on out of her back door. She would make these frozen treats called "icebergs," which were essentially Kool-Aid in Dixie cups with ice-pop sticks. She had all the flavors, from cherry and watermelon to lemon-lime and "blue," which she'd sell to all the neighborhood kids for 25 cents. This was the spot to go after riding your bike all day or playing ball for hours, and it created community among the kids and gave our neighborhood a real sense of character.

Now, I absolutely have no problem with a big ole frozen bar of processed fructose, artificial flavor, and red dye 40 every now and then. It reminds me of the summers of my childhood. But as a chef, and more importantly as the parent of four young people, I prefer to apply Miss Molly's method to fresh juices. *Note:* You'll need to freeze the icebergs for 24 hours, so plan ahead.

MAKES SIX 8 OZ [240 ML] ICEBERGS   In a food processor, purée the watermelon until super smooth and watery.

Pour the juice into the cups, cover each with aluminum foil, and poke the ice-pop sticks through the foil to center them in the cup. Freeze for 24 hours.

When the juice is rock solid, you are ready to go.

FUNNEL CAKE

1¼ cups [175 g] all-purpose flour

1 tsp baking powder

½ tsp kosher salt

2 eggs, separated

6 Tbsp [90 g] granulated sugar

Canola oil, for frying

Confectioners' sugar, for sprinkling

Funnel cakes aren't one of those plated affairs you bring to the center of the table. Everything from cooking to eating needs to happen while gathered around a Dutch oven in the kitchen. As kids, my cousins and I would trade off responsibilities—one of us would use a spoon to drizzle the batter into the hot oil, another would dust the finished cake with confectioners' sugar, and another would get to eat it while we'd wait for the next batch to emerge.

Not that funnel cakes are only a kiddie treat. Grandpop was a big fan as well, especially when they were paired with black coffee (no sugar or cream, ever). From the moment you woke up you could smell his percolator brewing, and it would stay on the stove all day and all night.

MAKES 2 CUPS [480 ML] BATTER   In a large bowl, sift 1 cup [140 g] of the flour with the baking powder and salt. In another large bowl, whip the egg yolks with 3 Tbsp of the granulated sugar and 1 cup [240 ml] of water. Pour into the bowl of flour and mix until combined.

Using a stand mixer or hand mixer, whip together the egg whites and the remaining 3 Tbsp of granulated sugar until they form firm peaks (they should briefly hold their shape before falling over). Fold into the bowl of batter and refrigerate for at least 30 minutes. Once the batter is chilled, stir in the remaining ¼ cup [35 g] of flour and pour into a piping bag or large squeeze bottle.

Fill a Dutch oven or heavy-bottomed pot halfway up the sides with canola oil and heat the oil to 350°F [180°C]. Monitor the temperature with a candy thermometer or a digital thermometer. Line a plate with paper towels.

When the oil is hot, gently squeeze the batter into the oil in a circular motion, making a couple of circles at a time. Fry on both sides until golden, about 30 seconds per side. Using a slotted spoon or a spider, carefully transfer the funnel cake to the paper towels to drain. Dust with confectioners' sugar and eat while hot. Repeat with the remaining batter.

MOLASSES COOKIES

6 Tbsp [75 g] shortening

6 Tbsp [85 g] butter, at room temperature

½ cup [100 g] packed brown sugar

½ cup [100 g] granulated sugar

2 Tbsp molasses

2 eggs, beaten

1 tsp vanilla extract

2 cups [280 g] all-purpose flour

2 tsp baking soda

1 tsp ground cinnamon

1 tsp ground ginger

1 tsp ground cloves

¼ tsp kosher salt

As a kid, I would sneak sweets into my bed and hide them in the pillowcases. Even to this day, I still keep cookies in my pockets, unwrapped, crumbs everywhere. You never know when you're gonna need a snack. Especially these treats from the best baker I ever knew, Aunt Sara Mae.

MAKES 2 DOZEN   In a stand mixer, whisk together the shortening, butter, brown sugar, granulated sugar, and molasses until fluffy, about 6 minutes. Change over to the paddle attachment. Add the eggs and vanilla and combine at medium speed.

In a large bowl, sift together the flour, baking soda, cinnamon, ginger, cloves, and salt. Slowly add to the wet mixture, folding together after each addition until well combined.

Preheat the oven to 350°F [180°C]. Line a baking sheet (two if they are small) with greased parchment paper. With an ice cream scoop, portion out twenty-four dough balls onto the prepared pan. Make sure to allow at least 2 in [5 cm] between them, as they will spread during baking.

Bake for 15 minutes, or until just firm and golden. Let cool on wire racks, then store in airtight containers for up to 1 week.

PEACH COBBLER

8 cups [1.5 kg] sliced fresh peaches

2 cups [400 g] sugar

2 Tbsp fresh lemon juice

2 Tbsp cornstarch

1 Tbsp vanilla extract

1 tsp ground cinnamon

¼ tsp ground nutmeg

1 cup [240 ml] milk

½ cup [113 g] butter

1½ cups [210 g] all-purpose flour

1 Tbsp baking powder

1 tsp kosher salt

Vanilla ice cream, for serving

In my opinion, this is the queen of Southern desserts. Food writer and historian Nicole Taylor once said, "If you don't have peach cobbler on your menu, then you ain't no Southern restaurant." I agree with that sentiment completely. Not only does it use a fruit that's grown in the South since European settlers brought pits to plant, centuries ago, but it also seems to show up during the most joyful moments for most Southern children, and it played a role in their happiest food memories. It certainly did for me.

SERVES 8   Preheat the oven to 350°F [180°C]. Butter a 3 qt [2.8 L] baking dish.

In a mixing bowl, toss together the sliced peaches, 1 cup [200 g] of the sugar, the lemon juice, cornstarch, vanilla, cinnamon, and nutmeg. Toss until the peaches are thoroughly and evenly coated. Set aside.

In a saucepan over medium heat, heat the milk and butter, stirring, until the butter is melted.

Sift the flour, remaining 1 cup [200 g] of sugar, the baking powder, and salt into a mixing bowl. While whisking, slowly stream in the milk and butter mixture, and whisk until smooth.

Pour the peaches and their juice into the prepared dish. Pour the batter over the peaches.

Bake for 1 hour, or until the crust is golden brown. Serve warm, with a scoop of vanilla ice cream.

EVEN IN STRUGGLE, DON'T FORGET TO EAT

Needless to say, Atlanta, Georgia, is where you'll find some of the best peach cobbler in the world. When I was in town filming a Super Bowl commercial for Tostitos, I definitely ate my fill. But those incredible food memories were accompanied by so much more.

On my way to the seminal soul food restaurant Mary Mac's Tea Room, I got to pass by Ebenezer Baptist Church, where Martin Luther King Jr. was copastor. His birth home was also just a few hundred yards down the street. I took a moment and stood in front of the house and just let the moment absorb me. I thought of the protests during the civil rights movement and everything that they fought for and were murdered for. I thought of all of the doors that Dr. King, John Lewis, Ralph Abernathy, Andrew Young, and Jesse Jackson opened for individuals like me. They've served as enduring, unparalleled, exemplary role models for Black men.

Not only has their legacy touched me, years later, but at the time it also shaped the lives of others in ways that endure to this day. Robert and James Paschal believed in the power of food to bring people together. And their Atlanta restaurant, Paschal's (which goes toe to toe with Mary Mac's for peach cobbler bragging rights), was the meeting place for civil rights leaders. It's where they'd sit, eat, and discuss strategies for literally saving the state of Black America.

Even after Dr. King was murdered, the restaurant remained a safe place for Black activists, who would often be allowed to eat for free. The Paschal brothers illustrated the ability of restaurants to uplift communities. Chefs and restaurateurs all over this country continue to provide sustenance and kindness to the leaders next in line to transform the world.

ACKNOWLEDGMENTS

First, I'd like to say that never in a million years would I have thought this could happen to me. With the way Black food has been thought of, at least in my lifetime, I had no idea that anyone might ever be interested in my or my family's story. The winds of change are blowing, and it's remarkable to witness what's happening in our culture: the stories involving the hands of the people who have toiled the land; slaughtered the animals; used the skin, bones, and fur; set the table; built the fire; cooked the food; cleaned the table; washed the dishes; pulled back the sheets; washed the pillows—and then did it all over again (and again, and again . . .). My ancestors were a part of it all. I am proud to stand on their shoulders, and I understand my responsibility to hold the torch proudly. I thank them, first and foremost.

I want to thank the "Three Sarahs" for taking me on this wonderful journey: my agent, Sarah Smith; my cowriter, Sarah Zorn; and my editor, Sarah Billingsley. Words come and go, but books last forever. A very special thanks to Sarah Zorn for bringing a wonderful glow and intensifying my words to bleed passion and wisdom and truth. I could have never done this without your guidance, your friendship, and your brilliance.

I want to thank my wife, Eugenie, and my children, Ali, Pearl, Caleb, and Noa. I know life with me isn't easy, and I am grateful for all of you and your love and support.

Finally, I want to thank the next generation of chefs coming up through the ranks. I admire your hard work and your dedication, and most of you are becoming worthy of carrying the torch and paying it forward. When I was coming up, there weren't many mentors of color, and I remember feeling empty and alone when I'd reach out to chefs who "looked like me." Just know that I see you, and I feel your work. Let this book be a way to know that I am always extending the hand of goodwill to pull all of you up.

Be well, everyone. Feed one another. Love one another.